Praise for
Joy in Teaching

"In this book, Dr. Carr performs magic! She takes what can be a taboo topic in education - teacher burnout - and breaks it down into a practical and research based light. Educators who read this book will finally feel supported as a whole person, with tactical tools to better their teaching, their students, and their life."

-Jessica Balsley
Founder and President, The Art of Education

"With *Joy in Teaching*, Dr. Carr has created an invaluable resource designed to give all teachers -- the new and eager, the experienced and hopeful, as well as those close to burning out -- a life raft of sorts to build resilience in the face of modern challenges. In this book professional educators can find a change agent leading to an awakened approach to what it means to live a life in education today. She offers real, research-based, actionable tools that all teachers can begin using today. As a future high school Instructional mentor coach, I intend to eagerly pass this resource on to all of my mentees."

-Rochelle Achenbach
High School ELA Teacher, 2018-19 Instructional Mentor Coach,
Spencer Community School District

"What incredible research and relevance Dr. Carr provides in *The Joy of Teaching*. Her examination of teacher burnout and resiliency provides educators with practical action steps and strategies they need to reclaim the joy in teaching. Dr. Carr guides readers through the process of reflection and helps bring light to the feeling of isolation in education. She empowers educators with agency to create change, improve and ignite their passion for teaching."

-Cassidy Reinken
Magnet School Coordinator, Cedar Rapids Community Schools

"I've been taking college classes since 7th grade, transitioning from student to full-time faculty. I've seen first-hand the benefits of learning from engaged, confident, and joy-filled educators. It wasn't until this year that I realized how resilient those teachers had to be when sharing their knowledge year after year. Noticing that I wasn't bouncing back after each semester like I thought I would, I knew I needed to make a change. But what change? Leaving a career I love? That wasn't an option. Picking up this book and doing my own homework, that of self-reflection, has changed my outlook and showed me how to reclaim the joy in teaching."

-Lydia Kitts
Professor at Union College

"Fifty years of being an educator, administrator and teacher has taught me that resilience is essential to surviving as an educator. Educators MUST have tools to help them educate with passion and zest, else they will fail both themselves and their students. Dr. Carr has done an amazing job at giving teachers the tools they need to build resilience, and administrators the tools to understand the issues facing teachers today."

-Dr. Diana Scroggins
Educator & Administrator, Myrtle Beach, SC

"What incredible insight Dr. Carr has in the field of education. Her personal experiences coupled with professional academic research makes this book an invaluable source to the educational world. It is about time teachers finally start to get credit for the hard work they do, while also recognized as human beings who needs their resilience levels nurtured every now and then too. I cannot wait to circulate this book around Ireland!"

-Jennifer Reidy
Founder of Compassion Fatigue Ireland

Joy
IN
TEACHING

Build Resilience
Fight Burnout
Reclaim the Joy

A Research-Based Framework of Action for Educators

DR. TIFFANY A. CARR

THROW OUT THE BOX

CREATE. INNOVATE. COLLABORATE. SUCCEED.

www.throwoutthebox.com

The book, in all forms, is available at special discounts when purchased in quantity. For inquires and details contact: www.tiffanycarr.com/book

Carr, Tiffany, A.
Joy in Teaching: Build Resilience, Fight Burnout and Reclaim the Joy

Published by Throw Out the Box, LLC
Mount Vernon, Iowa
Design (cover and interior) and editing by Throw Out the Box, LLC
www.throwoutthebox.com

ISBN: (paperback) 978-0-9998666-0-3
ISBN: (ebook) 978-0-9998666-1-0

Contents

The companion to this book is available now

Get the most out of Joy in Teaching

The Definitive Joy in Teaching Workbook guides readers, book studies, and professional development groups with extended discussions, exclusive activities, thoughtful reflections, and fillable resources that follow the book chapter-for-chapter.

Available now on www.amazon.com

To my family for being my everything.
To my husband, Steve, for his support and unwavering
confidence in me.
To my boys, Holden and Sayer, for inspiring me to create a better
future.

And for all the teachers out there treading water.

*P*reface

The road to this book is paved with personal discoveries and professional revelations.

I always wanted to be a teacher. In my time in education, I have had the privilege of teaching all levels, from kindergarten to graduate school, and I found joy in them all. However, a couple of years ago I reached a turning point in my career. After over a decade and a half in the profession I love, that I am dedicated to and passionate about, I began to question my place. Excitement was replaced with dread and my nights grew sleepless as I wondered if teaching was my real purpose. I lost my true north and everything began to move out of focus.

It was during this dark time that I began to reach out to my colleagues. I opened up about my feelings, and they did too - we shared stories, laughter, and tears. What I came to realize through these conversations was that my discontent with a profession that I still believed in, still loved, and wanted to find joy in again was not isolated. Educators all around me felt similarly. I thought back to those I have known over the years, who decided to leave the profession, and those I knew now that were considering it – everything came back into focus. I recognized that this affliction, this unspoken epidemic was big, really BIG. It renewed a spark in me – I became impassioned with discovering paths to resilience and bringing to light the issues related to teacher stress, overwhelm, and burnout.

Extensive research and a re-examination of what living a life in education means followed this renewal. Seeing educators at all stages of their career begin to question their position and purpose made clear a need for a practical approach to resilience within the education profession.

This book is just that.

DETERMINATION TO CHANGE

What I have discovered in both my personal and professional lives is that the 5-year process of earning my doctorate in Teaching and Learning trained me to approach problems with an analytical eye. So, as I developed an approach to altering what seemed to be the inevitable stress in my teaching career, I used my experience as a researcher and academic.

As I began to research teacher stress and frustration, I also delved into teacher burnout, lack of job retention, compassion fatigue, vicarious trauma, and the upcoming, inevitable teacher shortage.[2,3,4] Strangely, there was comfort in the statistics because it confirmed that I was not alone.

Too often schools do not emphasize support or do not encourage teachers to discuss their well-being, and because of that, when I found myself peering over the ledge of overwhelm and potential burnout, I had no sense that I was part of a trend. But, through researching this topic, which then became research for this book, I realized that I embodied these statistics and this normalized my feelings.

It also fired me up.

MOTIVATION TO MOVE FORWARD

The numbers of caring and dedicated teachers who felt like they were losing their passion and who were not supported in their struggles motivated me. During this time, I began talking face-to-face with educators, both teachers and administrators. Speaking with fellow educators about their experiences and struggles came easy. Everyone was willing to share and discuss their stresses and frustrations, their feelings of self-doubt and burnout, because they rarely had opportunities to speak openly. These conversations inspired me, made me realize I am passionate about teachers, and motivated me to develop strategies and outreach to support them.

This book, in many ways, is my passion project. I respect teachers and the institution of education. Education is a complex system, and despite its current and impending flaws, it remains steadfastly our privileged opportunity to make a positive impact on the future. And, teachers remain an undervalued and often-neglected pillar within this system.

In this book, written for teachers, administrators, and pre-service teachers alike, I have laid out methods and provided tools that will boost teacher resilience, reduce job-related stress, and support retention in the schools. I hope that this book is utilized privately by educators who seek to strengthen their professional disposition and also used as part of professional development in schools that recognize the need to support staff and build teacher resilience.

Dr. Tiffany Carr

*I*ntroduction

This is not a self-help book. Nor is it a book complaining about the state of education. It does not offer pity or pandering.

This is a book to inspire reflection, to motivate action. This is a book for educators who see the need for a new approach to teaching for their students and themselves. Who want to know they are not alone when teaching becomes stressful, when the profession they have dedicated their lives to begins to lose its joy. It is a beacon of light amidst the turbulent turmoil of a profession which statistics prove can devour.[1]

This book is a positive source of actionable and inspirational resources to support educators and help them to reclaim the joy in teaching.

NAVIGATING THIS TEXT

This book is designed for a variety of uses and for educators at all levels. With that in mind, an overview of what this book offers will help you to navigate your way and achieve the greatest results.

Throughout this book (the tangible, turn-the-pages-with-your-hand version) you will find symbols of compasses or map pins followed by bold text. These highlighted sections are meant to draw your attention and become talking points in discussions. The cartographic symbolism – in reference to realigning to your "true north".

If you are reading this book in a group, a book study (in or out of a school setting) or as part of a larger professional development initiative, there is a chapter overview at the beginning. You can think of the overviews as the objectives for each chapter. These can be helpful in deciding how to tackle the chapter as a group. You will also find discussion questions at the end of each chapter. The author suggests that each reader develops their personal responses before sharing – this encourages richer, meaningful discussions.

If you happen to be reading this book on your own, read it however you please. And, if it resonates with you, please be sure to review online and share with others who could benefit from building resilience and reclaiming the joy in teaching.

This book has a companion, *The Definitive Joy in Teaching Workbook*. The Workbook follows along with the book. It lays out reflection questions, along with individual and/or group exercises and action steps for each chapter. There is space to write and reflect as you move through the book. The Workbook helps facilitate professional development by giving readers activities and talking points for discussion. If you are reading this and wish to learn more about *The Definitive Joy in Teaching Workbook*, please visit the publisher's page, there are discounted group rates if you interested in a set for professional development.

GETTING STARTED

Teaching is a profession filled with some of the most caring and giving people in the world. Teachers willingly take on many roles and devote themselves wholeheartedly to our children and our future. We owe our teachers a great deal.

The rewards of teaching are immeasurable, but often it is not without sacrifice. Teachers face increasing pressures at all levels. Teaching is a demanding profession. Each year more and more is added.

High-stakes testing. Strenuous schedules. New initiatives. Higher demands. Fewer benefits. Less trust. This doesn't even include the expectations of day-to-day relationships, management, and accountability.

 Teachers are entrusted with our future. It's time their well-being is a priority.

It is no secret that there is a national teacher shortage in the United States. The high level of teachers leaving the classroom, many in the early years of their career, matched with fewer college students choosing to enter the profession, spell out a dire future for the field of education.[2,3,4] If you are reading this, you are most likely somehow invested in education and want teaching to be an attractive and desirable field. You also know the reality of the teaching profession - that there is so, so much more to do than just teaching.

No one benefits from frustrated or burned-out teachers. However, the benefits from happy, caring, strong teachers are immense.

AN EXAMINED LIFE IN EDUCATION

Awareness and reflection are critical pieces in the ability of educators to build resilience.[5] However, just saying this or knowing it doesn't help. Teachers often know they need to make a change to experience the joy in teaching fully. However, there are roadblocks. And these roadblocks often stand between the actions that educators can take and the professional development they need.

Teachers need time, space, and motivation to reclaim their joy in teaching.

TIME

A recurring theme within research on teacher burnout and attrition is time. Teachers work within intense schedules and often feel a lack of ownership of their own time. Many aren't able to eat or use the bathroom when they want to or need to. There never is enough time to get everything done. And, in light of the increase in staffing shortages teachers are being called upon to cover each other when substitutes are unavailable.[6] Time is our most valuable asset, and teachers seem to be always left wanting.

Educators need time to reflect and to course-correct if need be. If a teacher has a challenging class or a tough student, if they are struggling with the curriculum or standards, or they had a lesson land flat or an evaluation that didn't go well – they need time. Time to consider how it could go differently and what their next step will be. On the other side of the same coin, if a teacher had a lesson go great or they have a highly-engaged class – they need time. Time to consider what factors are causing the success and how they can apply it in the future.

 If teachers are continuously stretched thin and never given the time to be reflective and gain awareness then they are unable to live an examined life.

SPACE

Space is another consideration in the equation of developing an examined life in education. Teachers need a space to be reflective. Teachers share rooms more and more often. I have both observed and experienced a wide variety of teaching scenarios that provide less-than-ideal classroom arrangements. Funding, scheduling, and availability are all real factors in delegating space in schools. However, consideration in allowing teachers the necessary space to develop reflectivity is essential.

Although many teachers have a space during planning time and before or after school there are perhaps even more that don't have the luxury of an area to themselves, moments of silence, or places to decompress and reflect on their practices. These spatial concerns impact student learning, of course, but also influences teacher's abilities to grow as professionals. If we want teachers to develop their skills as reflective and adaptable professionals, we need to provide them the space to do so.

MOTIVATION

When teachers are left, time stretched thin, wheels spinning – they can lose the joy in teaching and lack resilience. They need support and motivation. Motivation is necessary for everyone and is closely tied to will. If we don't have the motivation to exercise, then it's hard to develop the will to get active. If we don't have the motivation to eat healthfully, then it's even harder to curb the cravings. Likewise, if we don't have the motivation to thrive in our jobs, it's difficult to develop the will to carry it out to the best of our abilities.

Teachers need the motivation to gain clarity, see their purpose, and to push forward with the insight of knowing their next step. They need to know that they are backed as professionals and will be afforded the time, space, and respect to develop their skills. And, they need meaningful professional development that demonstrates the importance of living an examined life in education and which gives them the permission to take a minute and reflect on their day.

WHY THIS IS SO IMPORTANT

Teachers, who have the responsibility of the world on their shoulders, need to be allotted the essential tools to be their very best.[7] And because of this, developing awareness and reflectivity is a pathway for teachers to grow as professionals and build the resilience necessary to reclaim their joy in teaching.

The life of a teacher is complex, and on the best days, you head home knowing that you have positively impacted the lives of your students and in a broader sense potentially bettered the world. Those are the days that you think about when you decide to become a teacher, those are the days they tell you about in college, those are the days you are teaching for, but those are not all the days. And those other days? Well, they don't get mentioned much, do they?

This book is for those days, and sometimes weeks, months, years… when it's hard to see the fruit of the seeds you're planting. It's about developing the resilience to be the best educator in the dimmest of times and becoming the light for others in your field. It takes reflection, planning, and work, but it's all worth it to reclaim the joy in teaching.

6

Part 1

Departure Toward Resilience

Chapter 1

Reflection

Chapter Overview

- Use inventory to reflect on your current view toward your position in education.

- Analyze responses to inventory to better understand where you have the agency to create change.

Let's be honest with ourselves for a moment. No judgment. No agenda. How do you feel about your life as an educator?

A loaded question. But it's important to begin here. To be clear about where you are, how you feel, and how you envision your career.

STAGE 1

No matter the stage of career you are in or what role you have in education - if you are a teacher, administrator, pre-service teacher, coach, aide, or substitute, it is necessary to understand where you are coming from before you plan where you are going. It is simple but true.

As teachers, we are encouraged to be "on," to show strength to our students and solidarity with our staff - it is rare in education, as in most businesses, to get personal.

This book is a toolkit and a resilience guide. To get the outcome you want, you must put in the work. It begins with reflection.

Self-Inventory

The self-inventory is designed to facilitate reflection and create a portrait of where you stand amidst the array of attitudes and perspectives in education. Try not to overthink. The best answers are the first ones that come into your head. Answer truthfully and privately. This is for your eyes only; you don't have to share this with anyone. You can find the sheets in the companion, *The Definitive Joy in Teaching Workbook* or fill out the self-inventory on a separate sheet of paper.

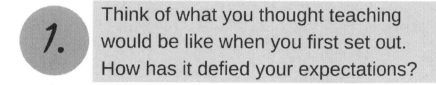

Self-Inventory

1. Think of what you thought teaching would be like when you first set out. How has it defied your expectations?

2. What school-related thoughts keep you up at night? Or, invade your mind during your "off-duty" time?

3. What do you see as obstacles standing in the way of you best serving your students?

4. Think of what makes you feel valued as an educator. List ways you wish you would be valued?

5. What supports or resources would make you feel as if you and your students were being set up for success?

6. What are your top 3 teaching-related frustrations?

For a fillable copy of this inventory refer to
The Definitive Joy in Teaching Workbook

ANALYSIS

Now that you have completed the inventory, leave. Walk away. Come back with a clear head ready to dig into what this all means.

.

.

.

Welcome Back!

Did anything stand out to you as you as filled out the self-inventory? Was there something, that as you wrote it, surprised you? Or made you realize a frustration or stress that you hadn't quite pinpointed before? Taking time to reflect on our day, on our practice, and on our reactions is a key piece in reclaiming the joy of teaching. Consider your answers as a starting point on your journey to build resilience against occupational stress and burnout.

Now let's dive deeper.

Step 1: Mark It Up

Grab a highlighter, a different colored pen or marker, or come up with some big bold way of marking your paper. Now, go back through your inventory and for everything you mentioned that is not completely in your control mark it up.

If knowing you are valued means an administrator tells you that you're doing great - mark it! If being a teacher is different than you expected because legislation ties your worth to your students' growth - mark it! If one of your biggest frustrations comes from a lack of support from the students' homes, you guessed it - mark it!

Go through every item. Think about how much of the responsibility for these items lies on you. Don't get too much into your headspace. Don't begin to think, *Well, if I were a more dynamic teacher maybe my administrator would take more notice. Or, maybe if I took more of an active role in local and national politics perhaps I could impact change in education mandates. Or, maybe if I became even more involved in the community and personal lives of my students I could influence parents and guardians to be more involved in their child's' education.* Don't do this.

Keep it simple.

What items are not in your complete control?

Step 2: Step Back

Look at your paper. I expect it looks a bit of a mess right now. Look at it as a whole and take in the amount of paper you marked. For many of you reading this, it is the majority of the paper.

All of those items that you just marked have weight in your day-to-day life. You have given them importance -some real, some perceived. You have allowed them to impact how you think of your profession and perhaps how you see yourself as an educator.

Just because something isn't within your complete control doesn't mean that you can't affect change.

What it does mean is that you can't take on all of the responsibility and subsequent baggage by yourself.

It is a common tendency of passionate and caring teachers to take on the weight of the world. That's part of what makes great teachers so effective; they are willing to tackle it all, go the extra mile, and never rest until they know they are doing their very best for all their students. Add to this all of the pressures due to testing, professional development, evaluations, and looming legislation. Year-after-year, functioning at this level can lead to exhausted and stressed-out teachers. These anxieties, frustrations, and stressors take a toll and are the strongest factors determining whether a teacher leaves the profession. [8]

The desire to carry this weight and take on the world in the name of students is part of the spark, the passion of great teachers. We must be careful not to diminish this spark, but instead, foster the resiliency to maintain it.

Step 3: Now Step Forward

The following chapters will address how to build resiliency by tackling the very items you have written in your self-inventory. Each of the items, the ones you have control over and the ones you don't, play a part in how you view your career in education.

This process will not add anything more to your already overflowing plate of responsibilities as an educator. What it will do is challenge your perspective and offer you new methods to examine what leading a life in education means and new angles to view your approach to teaching and learning.

*D*iscussion *Q*uestions

1. If you were just beginning your career in education, what advice would you give yourself?

2. What items from the self-inventory that are under your control, can you act on to improve today? What is stopping you?

3. How can recognizing which frustrations are out of your control impact your perspective on your position as a teacher and leader?

*C*hapter *2*

Impact of Teacher Well-being

*C*hapter *O*verview

- Learn about research that positions teacher well-being as a priority.

- Discover how the occupational stress of a career in education spirals and impacts students and schools.

Today, teachers are expected to assume many different roles, take care of a wide variety of needs, meet a mounting level of mandates, and demonstrate measured growth in student data. However, we rarely discuss the level of occupational stress teachers are under. And, we seldom take time to understand the impact that stress can have within the classroom.

RESEARCH INTO WELL-BEING

In the preface, I mentioned doing research, first for my benefit, and then to help others. There were a few research pieces that stood out to me then that fueled me to get to where I am now. These are important to note, as they put into context the importance of teacher resiliency.[9]

Very simply, I came across three pieces of research that drew clear links to what I saw in schools. These studies clicked together in my mind and took on a new shape. The links between these three studies, albeit obvious once laid out, make a strong case for the need for resiliency development and support for our teachers.

#1 Teacher and Student Well-Being

The first study, published in *Social Science and Medicine*, linked teacher well-being with student well-being.[10] Specifically, occupational teacher stresses resulting in a rise in student cortisol levels -often called the "stress hormone". The study was done by testing teacher burnout levels using an established inventory and then collecting and measuring student cortisol levels these tests clearly laid out a correlation between teacher and student stress.

This connection makes absolute sense. If you have a classroom where teachers are stressed, it's not a big jump to see how this could result in stressed students. Occupational stressors on teachers are numerous, coming from intense schedules, lack of autonomy, limited bathroom and lunch times, and mounting responsibilities and accountability. Teachers worry about their students, struggle to connect with parents, and attempt to balance interpersonal matters, all while being expected to maintain the sunny disposition of the ideal teacher. Sometimes this balancing act can be overwhelming.

This study drew concrete lines between the occupational stress of teachers, their level of burnout, and the impact of that stress on the well-being of both the educators and the students. Teachers who were on the high end of the spectrum for burnout reported more stress, less effective teaching and classroom management, were less connected to their classes and less satisfied with their work.

So, applied to school, this means, if you have stressed teachers you have stressed kids. One could also gather from the conclusions of this study, that if you have energized and engaged teachers you will likely have more energized and engaged students. Much like our expectations, the students will raise or lower themselves to meet our level of well-being.

This research piece was significant because it confirmed what I saw in my school, what I was hearing from administrators, teachers, and students. I have taught in a lot of schools, well over a dozen, and I can attest to the fact that when you walk into some schools, the stressed culture and climate is nearly palpable. Conversely, there are some schools that you can tell are positive and supportive after your first stroll down the hall.

 Teacher stress can equal student stress and the well-being of teachers impacts the well-being of students.

#2 Teacher Well-Being and Student Achievement

The first research nicely coincided with the next piece I came across, which made a direct link between teacher well-being and student achievement.[11] This research, conducted with 24,100 elementary and secondary staff, found that classroom teachers' well-being is associated with a range of measures of pupil performance. This was evident even after controlling for other related factors. It all began to come together. You have a stressed teacher; this leads to stressed kids, which leads to lower academic achievements.

This finding is powerful information. Teachers' well-being directly impacts student performance. Teachers who are often stressed are either a bit high-strung or a bit too lax depending on which way their survival skill swing, sort of a teacher version of fight-or-flight. In either scenario, you can understand how this could translate to student performance. A student isn't going to thrive in an environment in which the teachers aren't thriving. They aren't going to be motivated to push themselves or become excited about learning when their teacher is neither motivated nor excited either.

The significant implication of these findings is that if we want to improve school performance, we also need to start paying attention to teacher wellbeing. How teachers feel on an everyday basis is likely to affect their performance and so, in turn, the performance of the pupils they teach.[11]

Surrounding students with teachers who do not have the tools and support needed to face the challenges and stresses of their position sets everyone involved up for failure.

Stressed teachers can negatively impact student achievement and teachers who enjoy their jobs can positively impact student achievement.

This research struck a chord with me because it reflected my situation at the time. I was witnessing and participating in a system that was piling more and more on teachers while the climate of the school was sliding, the academic achievements of the students were slipping, and from both the inside and outside it appeared that the school was drowning. However, what couldn't be seen from the outside was all the teachers still treading water. There were teachers still trying to make positive connections and still hoping for the "pendulum to swing back".

At this same time, cumulative standardized test scores were published, schools were given grades, and teachers and administrators were categorized by these lowering achievement measures. And what do you think began to happen to those teachers still treading water and still hoping for that pendulum swing? One-by-one these dedicated teachers stopped. It is heartbreaking when teachers who care so much and are so passionate about being of service to others started to disengage. And, perhaps worse than that, it appeared to be contagious.[12]

#3 Teacher Well-Being and School Success

The final piece in my trilogy of "ah-ha!" research made it crystal-clear that I needed to pursue a path towards resilience. The article, published in *Educational and Child Psychology*, connected teacher well-being with the ability of a school to meet the needs of students.[13] It described the importance of promoting teacher well-being through consistent professional development. It demonstrated the need for strong teacher resilience training due to the impact of teacher well-being on the school's ability to meet the needs of diverse populations. And it even went on to postulate that an investment in teacher well-being would equate to reduced numbers of students that require external and internal supports and interventions in both social and behavioral areas. This is a strong statement, and one that, when you take a moment and think about it, makes perfect sense. A school full of disengaged, stressed teachers is not going to become the foundation for a welcoming and supportive learning experience.

This study, to me, was the final straw. It made the whole picture come into focus. I was witnessing teachers who I knew were effective and who were once impassioned by the idea of teaching disengage from their careers. It became crystal clear to me that a change was in order. If the well-being of teachers is not a priority, they will not be able to respond effectively to the day-to-day challenges faced in a classroom. These research-based findings, coupled with the culture and climate of schools, made it abundantly clear that it was time save the teachers.

 If we really are behind our students and want them to succeed, we also have to be behind teachers and support their well-being by building resilience.

RESEARCH-BASED EVIDENCE

Three studies. Separately they speak to the challenging and demanding educational landscape that teachers navigate each day, but together they state a need, a research-based argument for the strengthening of teacher resiliency. Teachers are the critical, pivotal force in providing students the safe and caring learning experiences that encourage them to feel happy and successful. Teacher well-being goes beyond attrition rates. Teacher well-being impacts students' and schools' ability to be successful.

THE DOWNWARD SPIRAL

You can see in the visual that stressed and frustrated teachers on their way to burnout are unknowingly negatively influencing their students' well-being. This in turn is lowering their students' academic achievements. Now comes the pressure of standardized testing, the threat, or promise, of emeritus pay, the accountability of all students without regard of their personal or developmental setbacks, the lack of bathroom breaks, acknowledgment, planning time, and respect and you have a serious downward spiral.

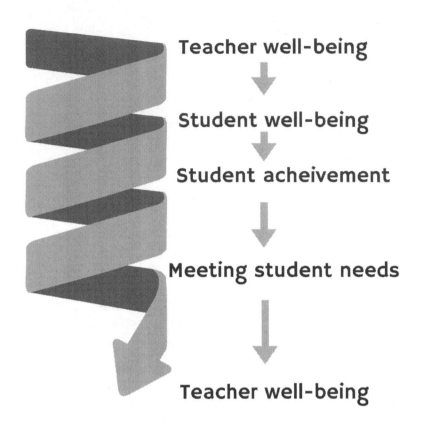

Teacher well-being

↓

Student well-being

↓

Student acheivement

↓

Meeting student needs

↓

Teacher well-being

Here's how this works: Each level feeds the machine more. The further down you go, the harder it is to claw your way out. Teachers' well-being impacts students' well-being which impacts students' achievement which impacts a schools ability to meet student's needs. This downward spiral impacts teacher well-being, their perception, disposition, and ability within their careers which then impacts their students' well-being and so on as the spirals viscously downward. Instead of building teachers up and giving them the resilience tools necessary to stop this spiral at the top, stress and pressures are added that accelerate the spiral. Is it no wonder that up to nearly 50% of teachers leave the profession within their first five years?[14] And the spiral repeats as it descends pulling down the teacher, students, and school as it goes.

Occupational stress and potential burnout can impact teachers' well-being in a variety of ways – it has the potential to impair physical and psychological health, reduce self-esteem and confidence, damage relationships, impact sleeping, eating, and can eventually lead in resignation and economic hardship.[15,16] Stress and excessive workload are the main influencers in teachers' decision to leave the profession, along with lack of support.[17] However, good teachers should not leave the profession because they do not have the tools and training to manage the occupational stressors they face daily.

By understanding the impact of this research and viewing the spiral we see a clear need to build resilience in teachers. The effect on student learning, teacher health, and school culture is evident. It is critical that teachers are equipped to face adverse conditions, adjust to a variety of situations, and able to teach strong.[15] For the sake of teachers and students alike, it is time to provide educators with the protective factors and resiliency tools necessary to embrace their positions, thrive in the schools, and reclaim the joy in teaching.

Discussion Questions

1. a. How do you recognize when those around you are stressed?

    b. How can those around you know when you are stressed?

2. When you are having a bad day at work who else in your life is impacted? How?

3. What role do you think a school should take in its teachers' well-being?

4. Consider the dynamics of where you work. What is in place to support teacher well-being?

5. Brainstorm initiatives or individual acts that would bolster teacher well-being. Which would be the easiest to implement this week? Rank them and make plans to do the easiest (forms located in the companion text, *The Definitive Joy in Teaching Workbook*)

Chapter 3

Burnout Epidemic

Teacher burnout is real.

It is devastating.

And, it's more common than you may think.

Nearly half a million (that is 15%) of U.S. teachers leave the profession every year.[18] If 15% of the population were to succumb to a contagious outbreak suddenly- task forces would form, research would be funded, and charitable 5ks would be run. However, the epidemic of teacher burnout is quietly removing caring teachers from classrooms without much fuss.

 Teacher burnout is an insidious epidemic and we must do something about it.

The causes are numerous. However, the results are the same. A teacher, who set out to make a difference with selfless intentions, begins to question their place, their purpose, and their passion.

THE BURNOUT SCALE

There are phases we go through as educators.[19] We flow in and out of different stages of energy and passion. This is normal, even healthy. However, there is strength in recognizing where we are and how we are doing, because only by arming ourselves with knowledge and self-awareness can we forge a path to a new level of joy in teaching.

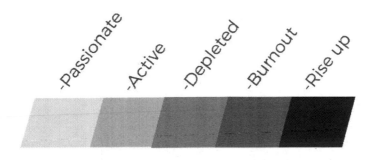

Teacher Burnout Scale

- Passionate
- Active
- Depleted
- Burnout
- Rise up

Stage 1 - Passionate

Maybe you are a new teacher or fresh from break, but you feel like you can do it all. And, you do! Reinventing programs. Problem-solving issues. Taking on new initiatives. Going the extra mile.

Need someone to chaperone that activity? Supervise that event? Take on that extra project? You're on it.

You have the energy to spare, and you pour it all into work. Others, who perhaps are not at stage one anymore can see your willingness to take it all on and add to your pile. However, you are fueled by the "a-ha's", and the recognitions, and "thank you's" . You see the difference you are making and it feels good. So good, in fact, that we may not even notice that our own personal (and protective) activities are fading away – the hobbies, exercise classes and socializing with friends are falling by the wayside in favor of getting more work done. It becomes harder and harder to find time to decompress and recharge.

Stage 2: Active

All that energy that we put in when we were stage one is now giving way to a bit of stress. The energy that seemed endless begins to diminish, and we get tired. Perhaps we daydream a little more, get distracted easier.

Meeting? What meeting? I was planning on grading. Where's Johnny? Did I give him a bathroom pass?

Perhaps we give a little less feedback to students; maybe we connect with them a bit less. We may distance ourselves from our friends and co workers, not talk about work as often. To cope with our change in professional outlook (and perhaps the loads of heavy situations we are managing in our classrooms), we may turn to dark humor or even mocking situations and students in our classrooms and schools. I see this most frequently in teachers' lounges. Perhaps it's not fair, but it is a way of dealing with what's going on.

The biggest danger at this stage is that we begin to change the way we see ourselves as educators, as helpers. When we begin to pull away, detach, or poke fun at what we once were inspired to help – it becomes difficult to see ourselves as authentic and caring educators.

Stage 3: Depleted

Teaching is taking its toll.

The demanding schedule. The heavy workload. The social, emotional, behavioral issues of students – some which we aren't trained or prepared to deal with.

On top of that: The lack of recognition. The lack of respect. The lack of energy. We wonder, *Where did our enthusiasm for teaching go?*

Everything blurs together.

What's hard at this stage is that we remember loving being an educator. We remember that first stage and the satisfaction we gain from being a caring and compassionate educator and we know that we really believed in what we were doing – it's just incredibly hard to access that now.

Stage 4: Burnout

In this stage, we are functioning in pure survival mode. We are going through the motions just to get through the day. We feel disconnected from the people and activities around us. There is little joy in the day and we carry that home with us at night.

This stage can affect us physical too, negatively impacting our health.

Burnout may feel like the point of no return, but it doesn't have to be.

Stage 5: Rise Up

When things get tough, it doesn't have to be the end of the road. It is possible to have the energy for teaching and for life after school as well. When we are further down the scale than we'd like to be this might sound impossible, but we can rise up.

 It takes a reexamination of school culture, a review of our own practices, and an understanding of strategies and techniques that we can use to reclaim the joy in teaching.

The reason I call this a burnout scale, instead of a cycle or a timeline, is because it doesn't necessarily have to follow in order. You can move back-and-forth at will. If you are at a Stage Three you have the ability to move back to stage one. If you are stressed you aren't condemned to burnout. With awareness of the layers of burnout and the factors that play roles within it, we can begin to develop strategies to take on occupational stress and burnout.

OCCUPATIONAL STRESS

The first step in fighting teacher burnout is identifying it before it becomes too much to handle. Occupational stress and burnout are two different conditions. Stress is common in most occupations, and for some, it can even be a motivating factor when it is perceived to be temporary. Feeling stress does not have to mean you are headed down a path toward burnout and it certainly doesn't mean you are not an effective educator, but it does mean that your job is impacting how you feel, and this should warrant some reflection.

Stress can surface in a variety of forms organized into five categories below.[20] It's important to note that these are all feelings of stress, not necessarily burnout, they can be short-term and combatted by stress-fighting techniques and strategies.

Anxiety

Anxious feelings can mean that we are nervous, uptight, even panicky. For some, it means a feeling of losing control, while others experience anxiety in racing thoughts or a sense of worry. Anxiety can also appear as a change in disposition toward negative thoughts and self-defeating self-talk.

Depression

Feelings of depression are sometimes associated with a loss of what once kept us going. A depletion of hope, decisiveness, confidence, motivation, even energy can be signs of stress-induced depression.

Physical

Stress can manifest in physical symptoms too, such as muscle tightness/soreness, gastrointestinal (GI) issues, headaches, agitation, and exhaustion.

Behavior

Our daily behaviors can be impacted by stress as well. Procrastination, withdrawal, impatience and the start of harmful habits, such as over-eating, over-spending, or self-medicating can all be outward effects of stress.

Relationship

Occupational stress can impact more than just ourselves – it has the potential to impact those we hold dear. Bringing the stress home can take a toll on our relationships in forms such as poor communication, disagreements, not listening to the needs of your partner, and anger.

Symptoms of stress have a spectrum. At early onset, they can easily be ignored or handled. To make a change, it takes an awareness of what you are feeling and a willingness to seek out the techniques and strategies that will best help you. The trifecta of time, space, and motivation discussed in the preface can be a positive part of combatting stress before it can mutate into burnout.

WARNING SIGNS OF BURNOUT

The hope is to not ever get to burnout.

The hope is to arm educators with the techniques and strategies to combat stress and face challenges with the tools to maintain joy in their profession.

The hope is to develop communities of support and cultures of understanding within schools.

And, the hope is to retain effective, caring teachers in their positions.

However, for these hopes to be reality we must prepare educators with the information essential to recognize warning signs and early symptoms of burnout.[21] The Maslach Burnout Inventory (MBI)[22] inspired this list - an established, research-based measure of burnout.

 If we can give teachers the tools to recognize the early signs and symptoms of burnout then we can hope to retain good teachers by offering resources, support, and services before it's too late.

Frustration

The frustration that comes with teacher burnout doesn't necessarily mean that a teacher is frustrated with students or administration. It doesn't even mean that it's the workload or schedule. Often the frustration of teacher burnout stems from an overarching feeling of not being able to really effect change.

Consider this: you have a teacher who is in the same classroom every day with the same pupils. They know what their students' need. They understand what needs to be done to help their students learn. And yet, they feel like their hands are tied. The heft of mandates, testing, and jumping through the proverbial professional development hoops takes its toll. Frustration sets in. And, the beginning signs of teacher burnout surfaces.

Lack of Personal Fulfillment

Teaching is one of the most rewarding professions in the world. You get to make a difference in the lives of your students and a tangible change in the world. You get to share your passion and help students find theirs. It is really one of the best jobs in the world (maybe I'm biased).

When the classroom door closes, the grading piles up, the meetings take over, and the testing mandates set in, it is easy to lose sight of the rewards of teaching. They say a teacher's day is never done - and it's true, there is always more you can do. This means most teachers sacrifice their personal time to get everything done. It is when the strain of feeling overworked takes hold that it becomes difficult to tap into those rewards and remember the personal fulfillment.

Overwhelm

Although this one is perhaps the most obvious of the warning signs of teacher burnout, it also deserves its place on this list due to the major impact it can have on teacher well-being. The sheer volume of work that teachers take on day-in and day-out is miraculous and also not sustainable - not in any real, healthy scenario. I speak from experience when I say that teachers rarely only put in 8 hour days. Drive by any school on any weekday, and you will still see a fair number of cars still in the parking lot far beyond school hours. Teachers often sacrifice their lunch breaks in lieu of getting more work done. And many teachers will work through illness because of the amount of extra work that is required to prepare for a substitute. The volume of work can haunt teachers. Hence teachers' gratitude for summer breaks.

Less Energy

Not only are the ever-mounting workload and the demanding schedule major energy zappers, but the other symptoms of teacher burnout can also be a culprit. Being overwhelmed, frustrated, having a negative outlook and not taking care of yourself is a recipe for feeling drained. This is the potential of teacher burnout - and it's not all just emotional - it takes a physical toll that can impact all parts of life.

This sign of burnout is dangerous because it is cyclical. As the signs of burnout creep in they pull energy away from teachers which result in less energy to forge resilience - which then, in-turn allows the grip of burnout to tighten.

Reduced Self-Care

When the signs of burnout begin to surface, it's often hard to see the forest for the trees. As a teacher, it is easy to see a sign of burnout and think that it's something else. For example - if a teacher is starting to feel overwhelmed - they may not recognize it as a sign of something larger and instead interpret it as a need to dig in, work harder, longer, and more isolated to get back on top. And, although sometimes feeling overwhelmed is simple - other times it can be burnout peeking out its ugly little head. And, burying oneself further into work will not solve the problem.

Teachers need the time, resources, and support to check in with themselves. Recognizing burnout and occupational stress is important, and is the only way we can begin to move toward the goal of stopping teacher burnout.

You are no good to your students if you let yourself burn out.

Trouble Sleeping

Sleep is an issue for many teachers. There are a few different reasons why sleep can become difficult for teachers. Anyone who has ever pulled an all-nighter, taken care of a newborn, or just lacked sleep can understand how a habit of poor sleep can take its toll on teachers

First, the nature of really, truly caring about your students means that when you aren't with them you wonder and worry about how they are doing. Did they really get that math assignment? Do they have a safe place to sleep or food to eat? On a quiet, dark night, the questions can be endless and keep you wide awake.

Second, the "what if" - teachers are responsible for so many different decisions that affect others every day that it is natural to question ones move, to wonder if you handled situations in the best way possible, and to replay the day over and over in your head when you should be sleeping.

Third. Stress. It's as simple as that. Stress can play havoc on ones' sleep cycle, as well as manifesting itself in a number of other physical ways.

Paying attention to what your body is telling you can provide you an early indicator of the potential presence of teacher burnout.

Less Social

There are introvert and extrovert teachers. Some teachers thrive socially within the work environment and some prefer to just get their work done. However, it is healthful to have "work friends", and it is important to be able to open up about the challenges and successes of your day. When sharing stops - whether due to the workload, embarrassment, or culture and climate that doesn't support it - it can be an early sign of teacher burnout. Teachers need to be able to be each other's support systems, and they need the tools and resources necessary to do so.

With a positive and supportive school culture and climate teachers can share with each other, build each other up, and problem solve issues like the true professionals they are.

Negativity

It's natural to complain. It's natural to have moments where it's hard to see the silver lining. But living under that cloud day-in and day-out can take its toll. Perhaps you know a teacher who always seems to have something to complain about (perhaps you are that teacher). This can be a cry for help - an early sign of burnout.

Negativity can spiral into an all-encompassing outlook, it can spread like wildfire amongst staff, and without the resiliency tools in place to deal with it - it has the potential to transform a school's climate for the worse.

RESILIENCE

It is clear why teacher resilience training should be an essential part of every school's professional development.[23] Teacher stress impacts more than just teachers' professional lives. Teacher stress and burnout spiral to impact student well-being and academic achievement, school success. It seeps into the culture of the school, it spreads like a contagion, and it affects the personal lives of those in its path.

Knowing this, we all should be doing everything in our power to build resilience. Because, if we can build teacher resilience, and curb occupational stressors, then we can not only hope to retain good teachers but, also create a better, more successful education experience for all.

THE VERY REAL DANGERS OF COMPASSION FATIGUE AND VICARIOUS TRAUMA

We have looked at the impact of teacher well-being on student well-being, student performance, and on the overall effectiveness of school. It is clear that the impact of teacher well-being is a key factor the educational success. However, it is also important to note the impact of student well-being on teachers.

As educators, our hearts are often heavy with the background information we have on students' home-lives.[24] We want to be there and help our students, and often do so at the sacrifice of our well-being. We stay up late worrying. We buy them what they are lacking with our own money (be that food, school supplies, or clothing) We go-all in emotionally and are invested. *All of this can easily lead to vicarious trauma and compassion fatigue.*

Compassion fatigue occurs when people in caring professions burnout from extreme mental and emotional exhaustion.[25] Compassion fatigue is a very real affliction that happens in education when we take on the trauma and circumstances of our students. It can rob educators of their "creative spark and spontaneity".[26] It strips us of our joy in teaching. It persuades us to question our purpose. Compassion fatigue can be a career-ender, and deserves a seat at the professional development table.

Many of the same strategies for understanding and dealing with occupational stress and burnout can be applied to compassion fatigue and vicarious trauma. This includes recognition of what is within and outside of our control, setting healthy limits and boundaries, and employing resilience strategies and protective practices. However, many find it much more difficult to negotiate the stress that they take on of others. This is

38

yet another reason why resilience education is so important for educators.

Awareness

As we acknowledged in Chapter One with the self-inventory, there are factors within the profession of education that may impact us but are out of our control. Although certain stressors may be out of reach when it comes to reducing occupational stress, we can begin to take control of how we let stress impact us. We can hope to retain good teacher by recognizing occupational stress and teacher burnout in its early stages and confronting it face-on with the appropriate resilience tools and resources.

Burnout is a real and devastating condition that occurs too often within the educational profession. This epidemic is a call to action. Teachers care deeply and give selflessly. They deserve support in building resilience. The focus of this book is to provide techniques and strategies to do just that – support teachers so that they may reclaim their joy in teaching.

Discussion Questions

1. What are some of the avoidable causes of occupational stress and teacher burnout?

2. What are some unavoidable causes of occupational stress and teacher burnout?

3. Who can we let know, and how, when stress and or burnout begin to take hold?

4. How can we support one another when we recognize early warning signs of stress and/or burnout?

Part 2

Paving the Road to Resilience

*C*hapter **4**

Begin Where You Started

*C*hapter *Overview*

- Take time to remind yourself of the reason you got into education.

- Review the top reasons teachers enter the field.

- Recognize the power of leveraging the cycle of the school year.

Sometimes it is hard to cut through the noise of the hurried school day to see the potential impact we have as teachers. There is power in tapping into your inner pre-service teacher, reflecting on your first years in the classroom, and reflecting on the decisions and goals that got you to where you are.[27] Taking a moment to reflect on your purpose is a simple resilience-building strategy that can make a big difference.

WHY YOU STARTED

They say you can't go home. However, there is value in reaching back to those feelings and thoughts you had as you became an educator. So, go back, maybe it's just a year, maybe ten, or thirty, or more – to that moment you decided to enter the field of education. Do you remember? You didn't just stumble into it. It took years of schooling. It took late night studying. Practicums, student teaching, job searching... You devised a plan, and you followed through. This is because you wanted to be an educator.

No matter your role in education, whether teacher, administrator, or other, you are who you are because you made a decision to enter education. And, there were reasons behind this decision.

Think back to why you started. What influenced your decision to become an educator?

- Did you have a dynamic and inspiring teacher?
- Did you have highly engaging classmate?
- Was there a teacher or administrator who was as effective as you knew you could be?

What events took place that influenced your decision to become an educator?

- Were you inspired by a spectacular lesson?
- Did have extraordinary extracurricular opportunities that helped to define your path?
- Did you have a memorable day in school that shaped your decision to enter education?

What subjects inspired you to become an educator?

- Did you strongly connect with a specific subject?
- Did you find your passion within a certain class?

- Was there a specific type of learning that spoke to you in school?

What did you desire to do as an educator?

- Did you want to positively impact the community?
- Did you want to make a difference in your students' lives?
- Did you want to share your love for teaching and learning?

REFLECTION AS A RESILIENCE STRATEGY

Take time to remind yourself of the reason you got into education. Why was it so important that you enter this profession?

What is your reason for teaching? Perhaps you had one strong reason, or maybe you had a long list of inspirations, either way reaching back to what set you on your current path is a resilience-building strategy that can make a difference. Below is a list of some of the top reasons people become teachers, what is on your list?[28]

Top Reasons Teachers Enter the Profession

85% To make a difference in the lives of children

74% To share a love for teaching and learning

71% To help students reach their full potential

66% To be a part of the "Aha" moments

50% Inspired by a teacher

39% To make a difference in the community

Chances are you had some lofty idealistic goals when you started out. There is no reason that those same goals shouldn't still inspire you today. The difference is now you are making those goals happen.

A study which implemented this strategy asked educators who had chosen to teach at disadvantaged schools and who were feeling the challenging nature of said schools, to reflect on their "moral purpose" or reason for teaching.[16] The teachers spoke of their desire to make a difference in children's lives. This was a key resilience-building strategy for these educators as it reminded them that they had chosen to be in their current positions because they believed they could and would do good.

 How we see ourselves impacts the way we feel.

If we lose sight of our purpose, we begin to see ourselves as someone who is acted upon, who has no control of the stressors in our life. However, if we take the time to reflect on the reason we are doing what we are doing, we will see ourselves as caregivers, change-makers, and people who inspire and give hope.

As the school year goes on it is easy to get bogged down in the minutiae. Days go on repeat. Meetings. Planning. Grading... Our world can shrink down to the size of a classroom, and we can forget the real and inspired reasons that we are in education. However, the recognition of the cyclical cause of occupational stress can lead to a renewed motivation to change as well.

THE SCHOOL YEAR CYCLE

Although each school year is unique, patterns exist within the framework of a traditional school calendar that seems inevitable. The more you teach, the more you become aware of the ebbs and flows that you will ride out over and over again.[29]

Mid-September is going to be a great time to try a new approach with students because you have already clearly established expectations and everyone is still fresh and optimistic about where the year is going.

Teaching the day after Halloween, when everyone's pockets are not-so-secretly filled with candy, is going to be challenging to say the least.

Parent/teacher conferences are going to add a level of over-worked stress to which your students will not be sympathetic.

Coming back after winter-break is going to require a review of guidelines and goals, but is an excellent opportunity for a fresh start.

February may be the shortest month, but within the world of education, it is going to feel like the longest.

May is going to be the worst time of year if you want accurate data or assessments from students (or teachers) because there is a mass mindset shift toward summer break.

And, this cycle – with many more milestones included, happens every single year, without fail. Even though lessons and curriculum may change, there is comfort in knowing what's around the corner and how to leverage it to your benefit.

Identifying that you are living this cycle can be a revelation. You can foresee the highs and lows before they happen. In a way, you can see into my future.

RECONNECT WITH YOUR PURPOSE

A powerful way to cut through the noise is to remember why you started and take inventory. It's time to dust off the original motivation you held close as you embarked on a career in education. Your inspiration is still there. Your goals are still intact. Only, instead of going into education because you want to make a difference, you can see that you are making those differences. You can use the cycle of the school year along with your reconnection to your purpose as an educator to boost your resilience. Your motivation to keep going is within you - and by looking back, it becomes much, much easier to look forward.

Discussion Questions

1. Think back to why you started. What influenced your decision to become an educator?

2. How are those influences/influencers still impacting your practices as an educator?

3. What are the times of the year that you know are difficult from your own experiences that you can prepare for better?

4. What will you do to reconnect with your purpose as an educator? How will others know when you do this?

Chapter 5

Community

Chapter Overview

- Discover the power of numbers through reviewing statistics on the toll of teaching.

- Consider your network of support.

- Learn the impact of a strong and supportive school community on teacher resilience.

Teaching can be a lonely profession.[30] Sure, you are typically part of a staff and a district. There are unions, organizations, online groups, etc. However, when the bell rings we inevitably close the door to our classroom and face both a room full of students and the challenges of the day all by ourselves. I know from my own teaching experiences that it is not uncommon for an entire day to slip by without speaking to anyone old enough to vote. Unless I sought out support or collaboration, I often didn't find any.

One stressor for teachers is that the work is never done. No matter how organized we are, no matter how many lunches we work through, how early we arrive before school and how late we leave after school, there will always be more work to do. So, it is not uncommon to get into a pattern of isolation. However, resilience isn't strengthened alone; we need community.

POWER IN NUMBERS

The feeling of isolation that can take hold as teachers begin to struggle does not have to happen. It takes only a glance at the following statistics to recognize that there is no reason to feel alone when things get tough.[11,31,32,33,34]

Statistics on the Tolls of Teaching

Teachers make an average of *1500* educational decisions each day - That's 4 per minute!

The average workweek is over *50* hours

86% report having insufficient planning time

87% report that the demands of work have interfered with their personal lives

78% report feeling physically and/or emotionally exhausted at the end of the school day

45% have considered leaving the profession due to pressures related to standardized testing

37% do not plan to teach until retirement site low pay as the reason

50% leave the professional within the first *5* years
1 in *5* leave with the first *3* years

These statistics – which at surface value paint a bleak picture of the teaching profession – demonstrate an important message that we must remember as we work to build resilience and reclaim the joy in teaching.

 When teaching gets us down, we must remember we are not alone.

When we are stressed, overwhelmed, or even questioning our purpose – We. Are. Not. Alone.

This is powerful.

Knowing that when we close the door to our classroom to face the school day and all it offers, that there are many, many others behind closed doors who are facing similar challenges and feeling similar frustrations gives us hope. There is power in numbers. We cannot ignore these numbers, and the stakes are high. Schools are beginning to take note, and hope reigns supreme.

However, hope is not action. The picture painted from these statistics is a profession that is hurting. A profession that needs support and is ready for a change. Research, statistics, and information all back the need for more support for teacher well-being and purposeful pursuit of resilience for educators. Building a strong community of support within the framework of a school is one of the most powerful approaches for resilience-building.

DEVELOPING COMMUNITY

The majority of an educator's workweek is spent at school, working on schoolwork, or thinking about school. Teachers will spend more of their waking hours during the week focused on school than on their own families and personal affairs. This, coupled with the previously mentioned statistics on the tolls of teaching layout a clear need to develop a positive and supportive community at school.

A common factor amongst resilient people is that they maintain strong connections with others.[16] Resilient people know that there are others who care about how they are doing and what happens to them. Forging these connections as a staff can make a substantial impact on the resilience of the entire school.

Climate

I have taught (and presented) at many schools. I can vouch for the nearly palatable sense of climate upon entering a new school. There is an immediate awareness of the atmosphere. Climate goes far beyond physical attributes of a school. It becomes apparent in how you are greeted at the office, how teachers respond to each other and to students in the halls, and the general disposition of everyone you meet within the school.

Perhaps you have felt this too.

What sense of climate do you think your school offers?

Community building through developing norms for communication, promoting positive connections, and offering support through resilience training can help to create a desirable climate within a school. These factors impact all those within the building, staff and students alike, and can be a force for change in helping to retain good teachers.

Communication

A key piece in developing a strong sense of community in school is positive communication. This means that teachers can rely on the established norms to know that they can voice their struggles in a safe and supportive environment.

Positive communication comes easier and more natural if you know something about a colleague outside of school. Think, how much do you know about your fellow educators? Schools have begun to actively encourage staff to simply learn about each other and get to know one another.[13]

As educators, we see the value in developing positive communication habits in our classrooms. This is why most teachers don't dig into textbooks and assignments on the first day of school. We want our classes to be a community, for students to feel they can express themselves in a safe and supportive environment. We take the time to get to know our students, their backgrounds, and interests. And, we do all this so that later, when the rigor of the school year sets in, we can fall back on the relationships built to help encourage and motivate our classes through the tough times.

We need to take this same care in building relationships amongst teaching staff. Building community is dependent on establishing positive communication expectations and habits. Creating an environment where teachers support one another and feel safe to express themselves is a crucial step in creating a resilience-building (and sustaining) school climate. It is as true within the staff as within the classroom, that when the demands of the school year set in, focusing on relationships and positive communication early will help everyone succeed.

Connections

Creating connections among staff builds community, establishes rapport and improves the overall climate of a school. Making connections doesn't mean that everyone you work with is now your best friend, that you're spending after-school time together, or that you would necessarily even be friendly to one another if you didn't happen to work together. What making connections does mean though, is that you know the people you work with well enough to feel a sense of belonging to your school. And, you have a sense of confidence that if things get tough, you have a support system to help you through it.

It is a fact that staff who feel a sense of belonging to their school communities and who feel connected to their students and administrators, experience less professional burnout.[35] This alone is enough of a reason to invest the time and effort to connect with your fellow educators. It is so simple. You can help yourself, and your colleagues fend off burnout by getting to know one another and being there for each other.

New teachers are given mentors and are set up in induction programs to ensure that they begin to foster this sense of belonging. These programs are established to protect new teachers from becoming another statistic of a teacher who didn't make it through their first years. However, for new teachers, it isn't enough to make mandated connections with mentors – their connections need to affirm membership in their educational environment, provide a sense of belonging, and make them feel like they are a valued part of the school and staff.[15] This is possible through developing connections with those beyond the new teacher's point persons. In a supportive community, all those involved in education, not just mentors, are there to welcome new teachers with open and positive interactions.

It's that important.

Your network of community stretches beyond the walls of your school and is inclusive of friend and family. However, your school community plays a vital role as they are the ones who are with you through the day, who truly may understand the challenges more than anyone else, and who can give you the most immediate boost when needed.

COMMUNITY, IN SPITE OF

Perhaps you are in a school that doesn't have a positive climate. That doesn't have supportive staff. That doesn't make an effort to establish connections or build relationships. Well, that doesn't mean that you are left without a life raft.

 When leaning on your community is not an option, you have to step up and take ownership of your resilience.

You know that teaching can get challenging, you understand that in the grand scheme of things the statistics don't demonstrate a positive portrayal of your chosen profession and maybe the deck seems stacked against you. This knowledge alone can be empowering. You can see the obstacles ahead and can determine your path around.

Yes, a community within school, where you spend the majority of your professional time is ideal, but for many teachers, this isn't an option. Online, traveling, shared, and distance teachers don't always have the luxury of being surrounded by colleagues. For whatever reason, if you don't have a network of professional support look beyond school to build your community.

Creating pillars of support is critical. Friends and family who understand the importance of open and positive communication, and who are willing to support you, can serve as your community. These relationships need a little more tending since those who you are relying on may not be aware of the challenges you face, however knowing that you can be heard somewhere and someone to give you strength can become the protective support you need in maintaining resilience and strength in the face tolls of teaching.

COMMUNITY STRENGTH

What a community does, that is nearly impossible to do alone, is it becomes a protective force in building resilience. Community can be the wall that holds us up when the wave of teaching challenge rushes. Community offers us strength whether the challenges we face are student behaviors, high workload, testing pressures, or one of the countless other stressors.

A strong and positive sense of community within a school, where teachers feel heard and supported, becomes the buffer between the external stressors and a teacher's internal beliefs.[17] Meaning that with the power of community behind them, a teacher can face challenges head-on without allowing them to waiver the teacher's sense of motivation and hope, or purpose.

Community building and support can make a significant positive difference in the climate of a school. We know and believe this, which is why we implement practices in our classroom that support community. However, many schools have not extended the same dedication to community to the teaching staff.[13] A sense of community can build resilience and prevent burnout. For teachers at all stages of their careers, working in a space wherein they feel heard and supported is a major contributing factor in their strength and success as educators.

Discussion Questions

1. What are the formal professional communities you belong to (networks, cohorts, committees, etc.)? How do they offer support?

2. What are the informal professional communities you belong to (those you choose to connect with about school)? How do they offer support?

3. Who can we let know, and how, when stress and or burnout begin to take hold?

4. How can we support one another when we recognize early warning signs of stress and/or burnout?

*C*hapter **6**

Culture

*C*hapter *O*verview

- Learn elements in boosting performance that the business world figured out before education.

- Discover the roles that both administrators and teachers play in developing school culture.

- Learn the key factors in establishing a positive working environment.

We purposefully strive to form environments that are safe, caring, and supportive within our classrooms. As teachers, we work to be sensitive to the culture and climate of our classes to best meet the needs of our students. The school, as a whole, requires just as much cultivating as your classroom, to develop a culture that supports all within.

61

Creating a culture of support can be a powerful force in retaining good teachers and helping them to reclaim their joy. Although, when schools attempt to address issues of culture they often do so by tacking on fragmented initiatives to existing systems.[13] By wholeheartedly making strides toward developing a supportive school culture for all we are taking a stance and stating, "Everyone can thrive here."

CULTIVATING CULTURE

Creating (or changing) the culture of a school is a complex endeavor. It takes planning, unity, and action. It requires a thoughtful approach to sensitive subjects. And, if done right, it can positively alter the experience for everyone involved. On the flip side, if a school does not choose to address the culture consciously – they have unknowingly committed to the culture that exists already.

 The culture of a school exists whether we take an active role in creating it or not.

The responsibility of building a positive and supportive culture in a school does not rely solely on the administrator's shoulders. It is a shared responsibility between all educators in the building and/or district. Teachers and school leaders are key influencers in their working environments, and as so, must take some responsibility for its development. Only by first acknowledging the role we play in creating culture within our school can we expect to create an atmosphere that promotes positive outcomes.[16] Reflection, communication, and planning are starting blocks that support the development a strong approach culture.

What is working for and against the culture of your school? By taking time to reflect on what the culture of the school promotes and how it is fostered, you can move forward in developing an approach to emphasize the positive and change the negative. It is important to keep in mind the goal: a desired, positive, and supportive culture, and not get hung up on the minutiae of the factors that feed into it.

It is vital to have a well-communicated and agreed upon plan in place from the beginning. A purposeful approach created by gathering the reflections and feedback of all stakeholders reinforces the community needed to achieve change. A unified front is required to bolster culture meaningfully, and having everyone on-board from the start demonstrates necessary inclusion and candidness.

The following graphic demonstrates key factors that define a positive working environment.[36] When developing a plan for your school, consider which of these factors are already in place and which require attention.

Key Factors in Establishing A Positive Working Environment

Setting high expectations to create a strong sense of community identity

Treating staff as professionals, with dignity and respect

Offering opportunities for teachers to affect their work through being a part of the decisionmaking

Recognizing and rewarding the efforts and achievements of staff

Scheduling regular opportunities for interaction and sharing with colleagues

HAPPINESS AND BUSINESS

Along with reflecting on practices, communicating with colleagues, and developing a plan to cultivate a positive school culture, it's important to stop and ask yourself one little question.

Are you happy?

It's a question that perhaps doesn't get asked often enough within the field of education. It's a question that we should ask more often and has the potential to offer insight into the current culture. And awhile back the business world came to a simple revelation regarding employees and happiness.

Happy Employees = Better Performance

Simple, right?

There is plenty of evidence that supports the fact that that happy employees lead directly to better performance and higher productivity and profits within the business world.[37] The same companies that showcase higher revenues, due to placing their employees as a priority, also have been adding new employees at a rate five times higher than the national average.

The key ingredients to creating a work culture of happy employees within the business world don't all translate to the education world - and we shouldn't expect them to - after all education is NOT business. However, there are a few essential aspects of fostering a happy workplace that are universal.

Fair Pay

It has been said time and time again, but it never gets old. Teacher pay does not reflect their work, dedication, and responsibility. Although teachers enter the profession knowing that it will never make them rich, getting paid a fair wage that reflects the education, professionalism, and tireless work that they do would demonstrate respect and acknowledgment for their work. According to many business models, this will result in happier, better-performing employees.

Great Benefits

I have been a teacher long enough to see the big picture of benefits decreasing. I have seen retirement packages, insurance coverage, and overall benefits cost more, be offered less, and in cases removed altogether. Teaching is moving the opposite direction of many high-level companies. The longer and harder teachers work it seems the less will be available to them in benefits.

Empowerment

One word that can change it all - *empowerment*. Businesses like Google are finding real tangible success with their model of offering employees autonomy and encouraging innovation.[38] Some teachers (including myself) have adopted a methodology into their teaching practices called "Genius Hour" in which class time is allotted to students to explore their personal interests and passions and then present their explorations to the class. Applying this to teachers, even at a much smaller scale, would demonstrate trust, professionalism, and undoubtedly result is some inspired ideas and happier staff.

Fun

More and more Fortune 500 Companies are reflecting on their work environment and finding ways to infuse fun. Having fun is a stress reliever. Having fun bonds a staff and refreshes them to face new tasks ahead. It doesn't mean forced professional development ice-breakers. What it does mean is a real culture of positivity and joy, togetherness and appreciation of each other.

THE ROLES OF ADMINISTRATORS AND TEACHERS

The culture of a school is profoundly influenced by how the staff and administrators interact.[8] This is a fact that we shouldn't take lightly. Educators have an estimated thousand "interpersonal contacts" each school day.[13] The quality of these interactions determines the nature of culture within the school.

 It is important for teachers and administrators to remember they are on the same team.

No one ever got into education for selfish reasons. It's easy to get caught up in our challenges – seeing what we need and how everything is impacting us before seeing the whole picture. However, proceeding under the assumptions that everyone is working hard and everyone cares allows us to approach concepts of culture with broader and more open perspective.

Here are some necessary culture-building concepts and a generalized idea of how teachers and administrators' views differ:[39]

Trust

Teachers- They want to be seen and treated like the professionals they are. They need to know that school leaders trust their teaching decisions and will support them. Trust is a key factor in building strong staff relationships.

Administrators- They want others to see them as serving the good of the whole school. They need their staff to accept that their intentions are to make the best teaching, learning, and working experience for everyone. Administrators need buy-in. Just like teachers need students to get on board to make progress, so do school leaders.

Meetings and Time

Teachers – their schedules are hectic. Their jobs are never done and when meetings are scheduled without a clear purpose and during high-demand times (like during the beginning-of-the-year or conference preparation), they long for more planning time and fewer meetings.

Administrators - Staff meetings aren't always at the discretion of the administrators. Often there are district and even state mandates that require the time of both principal and staff. No principal started their career to hold meetings and often the primary purpose of getting everyone together is to inform and motivate the staff.

Communication

Teachers – They need to feel acknowledged. This doesn't apply to just some teachers, some of the time. This is universal. Many teachers are underappreciated, under-respected, and overworked, and everyone appreciates having their hard work recognized. Whether it is a note in the mailbox, a comment in the hall, a chat in the office, or even an email – recognition is a crucial culture-building concept.

Administration - Like any leader, being the last to know the ship is going down is not the place an administrator wants to be. Therefore, when legitimate issues arise or something just isn't going well, communication is a must.

Leadership

Teachers - They appreciate autonomy. They want to be, and should be, decision-makers in their classrooms. They handle a lot, much more than any outside observer can fathom, but they also need to know that their administrator is there. When it comes to serious infractions, major incidents, and escalated conflicts, teachers want the school leader to take a stand, be the bad guy/girl, and back them.

Administrators - their job can be a lot - and from an outsider's perspective it's hard to see the number of plates spinning at once. Principals want to know that when they are called away to handle an issue that everything will still run fine. They want to have faith in their staff to work autonomously and carry on in their absence - knowing they would rather be there.

Hard Work and Empathy

Teachers and administrators share many things in common. Beyond their passion for the success of their students - they both have hard jobs. They are often tired, but they show up every day, ready to take it on. They build bridges, develop relationships, and work tirelessly. They do this because they care deeply and want everyone to succeed. Being empathetic to the plight of our fellow educators, whether teacher, administrator, or support staff, creates a solid platform from which to approach a positive culture.

TEACHER RECOGNITION

I want to take a moment to emphasize the importance of the acknowledgment and recognition of teachers. They are pivotal factors in establishing a positive working environment, and essential pieces in fostering good communication between teachers and administrators. But, it goes even deeper.

As teachers, we often make an extra effort to celebrate the successes of our students. We do so because we understand the impact of recognition. It is clear to us that our acknowledgment of their accomplishments positively impacts how they view their potential and their school experience.

The same is very much true for teachers. Teachers begin to feel underappreciated and unsuccessful when they continually face apathy from stakeholders in the community and at school.[8] These negative feelings can impact the way teachers view their profession, their potential, and their school experience. However, a school culture that regularly acknowledges individuals for their efforts and accomplishments can positively impact teacher self-efficacy and retention.

 Teachers need to see themselves as someone that can effect change and be successful.

Teachers' view of themselves cannot be, and should not be, wrapped up in data points and test scores. Successes should be inclusive of shaping behaviors, encouraging positive attitudes, and advocating for programs.[15] If we are moving toward a positive culture, we must also place value on those who help foster it. The recognition of teacher successes is a necessary component of building resilience, because, teachers whose efforts are acknowledged and reinforced are better able to take on new challenges, see themselves as change-agents, and forge ahead when faced with discouragement. Although teachers experience intrinsic rewards, outward appreciation can go a long way in promoting positive culture and teacher resilience.

NEW TEACHERS

New teachers to a building can infuse much-needed energy into a staff. First-year teachers are typically filled with idealistic optimism and fresh ideas. And, those initial years of teaching often lay the foundation for the succeeding years.[40] However, those first years are also rife with growing pains. As any veteran teacher can vouch for, there is a lot of learning-on-the-job that happens in the first few years. Which is why building a strong culture of support is so necessary in the plight of retaining new teachers.

Teachers enter the profession with an expectation that they will form emotional ties with their students and colleagues.[41] They want to make a change, and they see themselves and their calling, as being able to effect change for others. A school culture that promotes positive and productive relationships can help new teachers navigate the challenges of the first years by positioning them for resilience. A culture that supports problem-solving, collaboration, and reinforces one's calling to make a change will motivate a new teacher to stay strong. Likewise, unsatisfying and negative relationships with students and colleagues in those formative years in the teaching profession can induce stress and reduce confidence. These connections between new teachers and their professional relationships speak to the impact of school culture on teacher retention.

Thoughtfully cultivating a school culture that supports everyone within it is essential in fostering successful schools and resilient teachers. It is also a significant piece in solving the crisis of teacher retention. If we can surround new teachers in a culture of support when they are most likely to question their purpose, then we can positively affect attrition rates.

REWARDS AND BENEFITS

Teachers impact their students' lives far beyond academics. They encourage and inspire their students to pursue their goals and exceed expectations. They build relationships, offering care and support in matters beyond school and often are the rock in a sea of instability. We know that teachers' influences reach beyond the school walls. What we also now know is that a teacher's outward emotions and motivation affect students disposition as well.[42] Knowing that a teacher's disposition impacts the motivation their students is a strong argument for an investment in positive school culture.

Understanding that teachers and administrators are critical influencers of the culture of a school speaks to the need to create environments that encourage resilience and support success. Supportive administrators and happy teachers foster successful students. A positive school culture promotes more than just good feelings; it nurtures good behavior, creativity, and problem solving.[13] It helps to retain teachers who may otherwise consider leaving the profession. And, it creates a working environment that is enjoyable.

Discussion Questions

1. What do you think a stranger to your school would think of your school's culture upon first visit?

2. What do you see as your role in developing a positive school culture? Are you holding up your end?

3. What are some key areas that you feel could be addressed more in developing a positive school culture?

4. What do see as an obstacle(s) to happiness within your position in education? And, what can you do about it?

Part 3

Traveling the Road to Resilience

Chapter 7

Throw Out the Box

Chapter Overview

- Discover how a classroom that supports innovation, exploration, play, and fun can influence teacher resilience.

- Learn how developing culture of creativity values the students and teacher as individuals.

Think outside the box? No. Let's throw the box out altogether. A culture of creativity and innovation with increased curiosity and welcomed exploration can do wonders for building resilient educators. Beyond the benefit to students, which are vast, once educators free themselves from the shackles of the traditional education model, "the box," they can cut through the noise of day-to-day challenges and reclaim the joy in teaching.

INNOVATION

Innovation is a term that in recent years has been used to encapsulate a wide variety of meanings. From choice- and project-based learning approaches to educational technology and even flexible seating. Often new additions to the field of education are labeled with the buzz word "innovative". It draws attention and perhaps even lends credibility. For the sake of this book, we'll define innovation in education as an approach to teaching and learning that promotes self-efficacy and boosts interest and engagement through connecting activities to real-world experiences. It can be high- or low-tech, in or out of the classroom. Tangible, like a new resource, or immaterial, as in a methodology or approach. In whatever form, innovation offers a transformative approach to education.

A teacher that promotes innovation in the classroom is more resilient. Educators experience increased feelings of self-efficacy when they are willing to try new approaches and are open to offering more differentiated learning possibilities. Developing a culture of innovation by peaking student interest by valuing their ideas and providing them opportunities to take ownership of their learning. All this coupled with higher student achievement spells out an increase in teacher retention.[8] This makes sense. When you have teachers who feel trusted to explore learning opportunities and can guide students' successes through valuing their ideas and perspective – you build strong relationships and communities. A rich teaching experience, such as this, offers educators the resilience they need to face challenges with strength.

EXPLORATION

A teaching philosophy that advocates for exploration in the classroom is healthy for both students and teacher.

 Exploration, the process of discovering the potential of an idea, can be the foundation of a resilient classroom.

Not always having prescribed outcomes relates directly to most real-world situations and offers students the confidence to develop their learning processes and trust their ideas.

A school environment that promotes resilience is one where those within feel comfortable to admit mistakes. In fact, John Hattie has established that an effective education model includes mistakes as an important piece of the learning process.[43] Feeling secure that you can admit when you could have approached something differently speaks to the quality of the work/school environment. And, a learning environment that welcomes mistakes as an inevitable learning opportunity promotes positive and trusting relationships.[13] Educators who support exploration in the classroom are positioning their students, and themselves, for success not despite the mistakes that may occur along the way, but because of them.

PLAY

Although most clearly present in early childhood education, play can be seen in some aspects of elementary school learning as well. In late elementary and secondary, glimpses of play remain in the planning phase of project work and in arts-based activities.[44] However, the pace and stress of current educational demands, mainly mandated benchmarks and testing, place strain on the schools which follow a traditional education model's capacity for offering such activities.

Play develops critical thinking skills as students adopt the role of the problem solver and work through the discovery process. Play provides many opportunities for students to learn through social interaction. Taking turns, learning rules, conversing, and even decoding body language are all skills developed in social play. Being able to work and communicate with others is a necessary life-long skill. An educator can help foster this skill by challenging students to work outside their friendships and by providing opportunities to discuss activities and disagreements in a positive environment.

So, what does play have to do with teacher resilience? Much like innovative and explorative approaches to education, play has a tremendous impact on a school or classroom's sense of community and culture. Play and children are naturally linked. When we appropriately supported play, it has the potential to positively affect everyone involved. Infusing play into the learning environment can be a transformative step in building resilience.

FUN

Fun. It's not a word synonymous with education anymore. I am not sure it ever was. But it should be. As an educator, you are a huge part of students' life. They likely spend more time with you than their own family on any given weekday. Letting your personality shine, showcasing your interests, and letting students know you is beneficial to teacher resilience and student success.

Fun. Play. Exploration. Innovation. These should all be a part of a career in education. There is value in not taking yourself too seriously. There are rewards in sharing about yourself with your students. And, there are benefits in bringing some of your out-of-school interests to school.

Teachers who actively enjoy each other's company, who can laugh together and make learning fun are demonstrating a resilience strategy.[13] Humor can shift the dynamics of stressful situations and position those who join in with more of a sense of control. There is power in fun, and it is an essential piece to strengthening teacher resilience.[15] Cultivating a sense of humor and being able to laugh are excellent methods for releasing frustrations.

CULTURE OF CREATIVITY

As Sir Ken Robinson states, "We have to think differently about human capacity."[45] The traditional school model promotes a particular way of doing things. It offers questions with defined answers. It is designed to produce binary thinkers. Robinson asks us to reconsider what we want students to gain from their education. What we want them to leave school being able to contribute and accomplish. And all answers lead back to creativity.

Robinson defines creativity as "the process of having an original idea that has value." And, divergent thinking as "[...] the ability to see lots of possibilities to an answer, lots of possible ways of interpreting a question." Teachers who promote a culture of creativity, who offers students the opportunity to learn through innovation, exploration, play, and fun and who value their students' ideas and interest are creating an environment that is both supportive and encouraging to all within. This environment builds resilience through community and positivity.

SUPPORTING INNOVATION

What this all boils down to is the quality of the teaching experience. If teachers and students thrive in a positive environment that values them as individuals, then they will be more adept at facing challenges. And, although teachers have a considerable degree of agency concerning their approach to their teaching and resilience, the matter is not only their concern.[17] School leaders and legislators play essential roles in providing teachers the best opportunities to create learning/working spaces that support resilience and embrace innovation, exploration, play, fun, and creativity.

*D*iscussion *Q*uestions

1. What innovative, explorative, playful, and/or fun learning opportunities could you expand to include other disciplines? Which subjects? What would be your first steps?

2. What colleagues/department could become allies in developing collaborative and innovative learning opportunities for students?

3. What school-wide initiative could encompass all disciplines to create an opportunity for students to innovate, explore, play and have fun? What would be the first steps?

Chapter 8

Get Personal

Chapter Overview

• Learn about the pressure for teachers to perform.

• Discover the impact of sharing about yourself at school.

• Use the survey to reflect on how you can bring your interests into the classroom.

Educators accept that there are certain hoops they have to jump through. After all, many of the mandates for public education are determined by those who have never felt the reality of being a teacher. Accountability tracking, data collection, and drawn out meetings can sometimes feel like an obstacle to the act of teaching itself. For some, teaching begins to feel like a performance. But we must ask, for whom are we putting a show?

And, what can getting really real do to transform the dynamics of your classroom?

THE PERFORMANCE OF TEACHING

Teachers are pressured to perform, and in some schools where student achievement is tied to teacher pay, there is immense pressure. Many teachers are feeling trapped under the microscope of scrutiny from society, government, community, and administration.

Is it no wonder occupational stress is causing more and more teachers to rethink their purpose and consider leaving the profession?

 We don't want our teachers performing we want them engaging.

We want them digging deep, building relationships, connecting curriculum, and making a difference.

But, how can we do that if they must be putting on a performance? If when someone walks by their classroom they are expected to always be "on"?

Maybe teaching and learning doesn't need to look "on". Maybe students don't have to look busy. Just maybe, learning can look all sorts of different ways and success can be measured by more than just data points.

Think about it. Is there a discrepancy between how you want your students to learn and what you want your administrator to observe? If so, we have a serious disconnect in what is happening in education today.

Have you ever felt guilty letting your students have fun? Have you ever closed your classroom door to hide your activities from passersby?

I once had a kindergarten teacher peak out of her closed classroom to tell me, and I quote, "Shhh, don't tell anyone, but I am letting my students paint today." It broke my heart. Kindergarteners should be painting. Students should get to work hands-on, learn from exploration and experimentation. They should be encouraged to try new approaches and feel okay with making mistakes because that is authentic learning.

Student learning doesn't have to look like a nose in a textbook, or a quiet classroom – in many cases it shouldn't look like that. Providing children time and space to reflect on learning experiences then following up on reflections with discussions and an opportunity to carry ideas and actions forward supports students in becoming skilled learners.

If, as educators, we want to prepare our students for the future and genuinely provide them 21st-century skills, then we have to be prepared to let go of the antiquated mindset of what is considered learning. We need not to feel guilty for allowing students to enjoy learning. And we have to welcome the world into our classrooms to show them that success in education can be unapologetically enjoyable.

GET PERSONAL

By sharing about yourself, digging into your interests, and letting your personality shine you provide students a way to connect with you and administrators a way to acknowledge you.

You can complete the interest inventory in the companion, *The Definitive Joy in Teaching Workbook* or fill it out on a separate sheet of paper. Often there are aspects about you that you never considered bringing into the classroom. Keep the inventory "G rated" and if you're with a group be prepared to share.

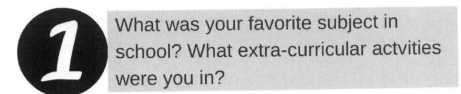

Interest Inventory

1 What was your favorite subject in school? What extra-curricular actvities were you in?

2 What is your favorite tv and movie genres? Any stand-out favorites?

3 What do you read when you want to be entertained? Magazines, websites, apps, books...

4 What is your favorite thing to do off the "grid", no electronics or wi-fi?

5 What is your pop-culture guilty pleasure? a YA novel, a pop band, a tv show...

6 What is the thing you are best at completely outside of teaching?

For a fillable copy of this inventory refer to
The Definitive Joy in Teaching Workbook

86

Take a look at your inventory list. Although these are your interests, this is also a list of your strengths. It showcases your personality and what you value and invest time in outside of school.

Sharing with Students

How much of what is on this list do your students know? How much of it have you never even thought of bringing up to your students? And what would happen if you did?

Consider what your classroom would be like if you could let your guard down just a little and played that favorite boy band song from college. What would your students say if you chimed in about the latest episode of your favorite zombie apocalypse show? What if you displayed that team pennant or action figure collection? What if you shared stories from when you got braces, were in the art club, on the football team...

 Sharing about yourself humanizes you to your students.

It allows them to see behind the veil of "teacher" and encourages engagement.

Sharing with School Leaders

Look again at your inventory list. How much of what is on your list does your administration know? How much of it have you never even thought of bringing up to your administration? And what would happen if you did?

The research on the significance of acknowledging student diversity and strengths is accepted into common practice. However, research also shows the importance and positive impact of acknowledging teachers' interests and strengths. This is especially true when it comes to recognition by school leaders.[13]

When administrators and school leaders take time to get to really know their faculty there is a ripple effect.

Teachers begin to feel more appreciated through the recognition and this in turn positively impacts their interactions with students.

Sharing with the School

Another effect of acknowledging teachers' strengths and interests is finding new ways teachers can belong to the school. Perhaps there is a science teacher who is really into video games – he could start a gaming club and connect with students who are not in any other extracurricular activities. Perhaps there is a kindergarten teacher who runs marathons during the summer – she could start a running club after school to promote physical fitness and comradery through exercise. Teachers may find new connections to each other and to the administrators and school leaders. And, just like with the classroom teacher, sharing humanizes. It builds bonds, it encourages engagement, and it opens communication and rapport.

Interests and Strengths as Resilience

Beyond all of these benefits of sharing your interests and strengths, whether it is with students or school leaders, it is essential to recognize the role of focusing on teacher strengths as a central premise of teacher resiliency.[40] The knowledge that their strengths are recognized and their interests are of value bolsters the ability of teachers to manage stress and navigate adverse conditions.

Interjecting our interests into the school day – either directly through organized extracurricular activities or subtly through jokes and references in the classroom - allows teachers to be seen through a different lens, communicate through a new channel, and develop resiliency through positive recognition.

*D*iscussion *Q*uestions

1. What are some interests you could bring into school to form stronger connections with students?

2. What are some interests you could bring into school to form stronger connections with staff?

3. What are ways your interests and strengths outside of school could be put to use at school?

Chapter 9

Planning for Resilience

Chapter Overview

- Learn a variety of changes you can make to your planning and practice as an educator to find more time and joy in teaching.

- Discover how knowing your strengths as a teacher can build resilience.

I have kept a planner each year of my teaching. I save them. At the end of the school year, I like to look back through all that my classes have accomplished. It's sentimental, nostalgic, and very insightful.

Let me paint you a picture of what mine tend to look like: the first month of school my writing is neat, small, and centered on each line and in each box. The pages are smooth, and I would happily share the planner with an administrator to demonstrate my preparedness. Fast forward to the end of the school year. My writing no longer follows the lines or agrees to be confined inside the boxes of my planner. Arrows, scribbles, and legitimate redactions pepper the final pages. The pages ripple from being spilled, on dried, and spilled on again. A dark ring from a coffee cup tends to be the pièce de résistance. My planner stands as a testament to the hurried nature of our profession.

We set out with the best of intentions to stay organized and ahead of the curve, but as the school year has its way with teachers it chips away at our intentions. It slowly erodes our sense of control. And, it does so without us even knowing. Meetings, conferences, and even more meetings eat away at our time as we dodge the obstacles of schedule changes.

 Teachers need a toolbox full of strategies that set them up for success.

Having approaches to protect our time and work toward our strengths can help us stay on track as the school year unfolds.

TIME

There are many stressors on teachers, however, most pale in comparison to the stress of lack of time.[46]

Come to the end of August; life turns into a mad dash of teaching, planning, organizing, emails, phone calls, meetings, and grading... with little time left for essential tasks such as eating and using the restroom. Priorities become strained, personal and family time shifts just out of reach, and before we know it our jobs become our lives. It's easy to fall into this rut, to let the endless to-do lists bury you... even if you know it's coming.

To get ahead of it all we need time. Time to develop approaches for active participation in classes, time to implement alternative strategies. And, time to reflect on the desired learning outcomes. These pieces are essential to maintaining a positive learning environment.[8] We can protect our time for what matters most by developing reliable approaches to obstacles that can potentially derail our organization and drain our time (see Part 4 for more resilience building strategies).

Say "No"

You've probably heard it before, but are you practicing it? Really. Try it. Say it. Out loud.

"No."

Say it when that parent requests a meeting outside of school time because they can't alter their work schedule, but they don't think twice about asking you to sacrifice your personal time. Say it when you are asked really, really nicely to take on one more duty, one more class, one more extracurricular, one more of anything that you don't believe is the best use and value of your time.

There are lots of great ways to say it besides just saying "No" and many ways to positively handle responses. Saying "No" gets more comfortable with practice.

 You will always put students first, but placing value on your own time will help you to be the best teacher you can be.

Your time is one of your most valuable assets and protecting it will help both you and your students.

Say "Yes"

As hard as it to say "No," it is often even harder for educators to say "Yes."

Learn to say "Yes." Listen to the voice in your head asking you for a break. You need to give to yourself when it is vital for your well-being, and this means saying yes to you.

So, say "yes" to leaving your grading at school tonight. "Yes" to a making it to the gym or going out to eat. "Yes" to meeting friends and leaving school behind for an evening. "Yes" to you. You will always make time for your students; it's in your nature. However, it's not selfish to place yourself on your list of priorities for the day. It is necessary.

 You are no good to your students if you are burned out – take time for yourself now.

The grading will always be there waiting. Always.

No More Teacher Guilt

Mean it when you Say "No" to needy parents and coworkers. And mean it when you say "Yes" to taking care of yourself and your own needs. Don't feel guilty.

There is an overarching social and cultural expectation that teachers have to be selfless saints that will endure the lack of respect and lack of compensation, the lack of time and lack of support and continue to give endlessly. This is not true.

You can be a caring, effective, and powerful teacher *and* also have boundaries, have a personal life, and take care of your own needs. This starts with letting go of the late night guilt sessions, lying awake and questioning if you could have done more, been more, given more.

It is a monumental step, and not an easy one, to resist the reflex to internalize it all. It takes practice. Trust that you are doing good by your students. It takes confidence in your value. And, it takes strength.

Set Up Systems

Setting up systems within your classroom that encourage independent learning will both provide your students a sense of ownership in their education and will promote a more peaceful teaching experience for you. By creating a classroom wherein students know what the next step of the process is you can spend your time developing relationships, scaffolding learning, and working alongside your students. This is true whether you teach kindergarteners or high school seniors - whether you teach science or English.

 Providing your students more autonomy frees your time up to enjoy teaching more.

Imagine if students didn't need to ask permission to continue to the next phase of an assignment or where to get a supply. By setting up systems within your room that empower your students to be decision-makers, you free yourself of being the gate-keeper and can focus on what truly matters.

Practice Being Present

How can not checking your email build your resilience? How can not having your finger on the pulse of what is going on every second help you save time in your day? Here's how. Multi-tasking is your enemy. Really. It is a fact that doing multiple tasks at the same time actually reduces productivity by 40%.[47] Shifting between tasks, especially tasks that take different brain power, such as teaching and clicking around on the computer, require you to refocus your attention in different directions and inefficiently taxes your brain.

Now, think about how much multi-tasking is involved in a single day of teaching, a single hour…

The average teacher makes over 1,500 decisions in a school day. It's one of those well-known statistics, like 50% of teachers leave the profession in the first 5 years. So, the next time you are tempted to wander over to your computer between helping students, question if it's the right move and refocus your attention back to what really matters.

Pick and Choose Your Extracurriculars

Stay involved. Be there for your students. But, do it with intention and value for your own time.

As a teacher you know there is a nearly limitless amount of activities that you can sponsor, coach, chair, and lead. There are academics, sports, recreational, and hobby groups, and as a teacher, you want to support your students and ensure that they have a place to belong and feel acknowledged and appreciated within school. You know that for some of your students the extracurriculars mean more than the academics, so it's important that these opportunities are available to them.

It is also essential that you can offer your students the best version of yourself and doing that often requires a reevaluation of where and how you spend your time and energy.

 Spreading yourself too thin or spinning your wheels in an effort to do everything only reduces your effectiveness as a teacher.

Do what you do best and leave the rest.

Formative over Summative

You might be wondering what assessment has to do with saving you time. The answer could be "a lot." Giving a summative assessment to a student formalizes learning. Students can become anxious, and you are left with a heap of tests to grade. Testing is an accepted part of education, but what if you could limit summative assessments and save your students some stress and yourself some time?

By utilizing a variety of formative assessments, you can keep track of your students' learning and not continually test them. They don't even have to know that you are assessing them. There are a vast variety of formative assessments from student-created checklists, journals, and logs to teacher-created activities, exit tickets, and graphic organizers.

 Your goal is to ensure students learn. Let students demonstrate this through means other than testing when possible.

You will have a happier class and less paperwork too.

Streamline Your School Bag

Do you remember in the movie *Mary Poppins* when she set down her carpet bag and proceeded to pull a variety of objects out including a hat stand, floor lamp, and a potted plant? Well, many teacher bags rival that of Mary Poppin's and can become a source of stress for both your time and shoulder.

Your school bag can have a impact on how you spend your out-of-school time. If your bag is overflowing with school work and you bring it back and forth from home to school each day, you never really are leaving school behind. If you are trying to relax and your school bag is sitting in the corner staring you down with work you know you could be doing, then you aren't truly relaxing.

Take a hard look at what you are toting around with you and bring home only what you intend on making time for. If it can wait, then leave it and enjoy some much-needed R & R.

Batch Your Work

Batching is a term that isn't used much in academic circles but is an effective way of getting work done efficiently and is considered a productivity hack in the business world. It involves grouping like tasks to cut through them quickly. You save time and brainpower by not constantly shifting gears.

Instead of moving back and forth from grading student work, to organizing your supplies, to writing plans on the computer, and taking time to answer emails and phones calls in between each, you linearly attack your work, completing one task before moving on to the next. When you focus your energy, you can accomplish more in less time because you don't have to refocus with each new task.

Batching sounds simple enough, but when you face with limited planning time, it's easy to get caught up in trying to get it all done at once. This approach often leads to a scurry of inefficiency - leaving work undone and you worse for the wear. So, plan how you plan and try batching your work; you will get more done and be more prepared for the rest of the day having saved time and brain power.

Planning Time, Tools, and Techniques

Teachers' schedules are hectic, and their work never ends. There is always a pile of papers to grade, lessons to plan, data to be collected, emails to write, and meeting to attend. We often sacrifice, time to go to the bathroom, to talk with other adults, and to eat lunch in the name of getting everything done.

The school day can take on different forms depending on position, grade level, schedule, and a variety of other factors. However, no matter what your day may look like, developing a purposeful approach to time (both with students and without) can make a genuine impact on how you view your profession.

When we set boundaries and priorities for our time, and come to the realization that we can't always do everything for everyone, it becomes much easier to view our position with a sense of control. The work will always be there, but breaking up the day and gifting yourself a moment to decompress, laugh, or even enjoy your lunch can make a positive impact on the rest of your day. Resilience comes in many forms and by developing strategies to manage and protect your time you can focus your energy on what is most important.

TEACHER STRENGTH

Teaching takes strength.

Teachers' strengths take on many forms and within each lies its own kind of resiliency.[48] If we can learn how to tap into our unique strengths, we can face challenges with greater confidence and resilience. Each strength carries its own power and struggles.

Determining Your Strength

As educators, we understand the importance of reflection. We reflect on the challenges and successes of our lessons, how the culture and climate of our classrooms are evolving, and the best ways to meet the needs of our classes. Reflection allows us to make better choices, improve our practice, and be better educators. However, school days are busy, and we rarely take the time to turn the mirror around to ourselves.

Nosce te ipsum is Latin for "know thyself."

It is as true and powerful of a maxim now as it was when it was first uttered centuries ago. It speaks the value of self-knowledge and the importance of being a reflective citizen.

By taking stock of our own strengths within the field of education we can learn to rely on the traits and abilities that will help us the most to become more resilient educators.

Self-awareness can be an asset in developing resilience. Knowing that you have strengths that you can lean on when the going gets tough can boost your confidence and sense of self-efficacy. Understanding where you tend to stumble, where your weaknesses may lie, provides insight in difficult times. The following categories are different teacher strengths. As with any superlative, we are never all of one and none of the other, but rather an amalgamation that has the potential to grow and change.

As you read through them, consider which traits make up your approach to teaching and learning and how you can leverage these qualities to be a stronger and happier teacher. Knowing your strengths and understanding where you might stumble allows you to face each day of teaching with confidence and resilience.

Teacher Strengths
(and potential struggles)

Consider the degree to which each of these strengths is present in your approach to teaching and learning.

The Organized Teacher

Systems, structures, and organization are where the organized teacher thrives. Their focus on preparation and planning allows them to face obstacles with a clear mind and a professional demeanor.

A plan for every situation and a place for every item is the organized teacher's dream, however, we know that teaching isn't always neat and tidy. The organized teacher can sometimes struggle a bit when things get messy and plans change quickly.

The Passionate Teacher

The passionate teacher harnesses their dedication and love for the profession to face obstacles with a sense of confidence and heart. No matter what is thrown at them, they know they can rely on their sensibilities and their instincts to get them through.

The passionate teacher is devoted to school and places their job as a top priority which is great, except sometimes carving out time for your non-work life, friends, and self can be a struggle.

The Multi-tasking Teacher

At any given time teachers have multiple plates in the air. The multi-tasking teacher smoothly juggles multiple while facing new obstacles with a sense of assurance and poise.

Although multi-tasking suites the teaching profession it is also proven to reduce productivity. Sometimes it's best to focus on one task and see it through to completion, which can be a struggle when you're accustomed to doing it all at once.

The Funny Teacher

Hey, is this thing on? The funny teacher, you know who they are or if you are one, makes those around them laugh which allows them to face obstacles knowing that they can disarm the situation with humor.

The funny teacher is great at easing tensions and lightening the mood, but when it comes to getting serious sometimes it's hard to stop being the comedian and buckle down.

The Compartmentalized Teacher

The compartmentalized teacher has the unique ability to leave work at work, which means that they aren't lying awake thinking about their day and their students like many of us.

Although the compartmentalized teacher seems to have mastered balance, it is when the work-life/home-life line starts to blend and tighter connections to school are available, he/she sometimes faces a struggle.

The Adaptable Teacher

The Adaptable teacher's ability to pivot and change plans allows him/her to face obstacles with a sense of confidence that he/she can handle anything that is thrown at him/her.

While the adaptable teacher may seem to be the picture of calm within the storm, they sometimes can face struggle when it comes to mapping out solid plans and adhering to rigid structures, which we all know are often part of educational mandates.

The Emotional Teacher

The emotional teacher wears their heart on their sleeve, and that's not a bad thing. Their emotional approach to their profession allows them to face obstacles with a sensitive and empathetic sensibility.

The emotional teacher can sometimes face struggle when the going gets tough. Although it's a great to be tender-hearted teachers need a thick skin at times in order to make it through the school day.

The Social Teacher

The social teacher's ability to connect with others, whether it be fellow educators or students, allows them to face obstacles knowing that whatever is thrown at them, they don't have to face it alone.

The social teacher isn't afraid to offer and rely on support, however, they sometimes face struggle if they are roped into gossip or negativity and their social tendencies turn unprofessional.

Discussion Questions

1. After reading Chapter Nine, how will you look at and manage your time differently?

2. What other teacher types would you add to the list?

3. Which of your strengths can you rely on when things get tough?

Part 4

The Journey is the Destination

*C*hapter *10*

Live What You Teach

*C*hapter *O*verview

- Discover the power of taking your own advice.

- Learn the reach of impact in fostering high teacher self-efficacy.

- Reflect on how defining your boundaries can help you be a more effective teacher.

Teachers are the heart of the school. Teachers represent strength, knowledge, and love to their students. They offer encouragement when their students are struggling and acknowledgment and celebration when they do well. Teachers wear many hats and have to be good at many things. However, one thing that many teachers aren't great at is taking their own advice.[49]

Teachers have a wealth of wisdom. They can often see how things will play out with students if they believe in themselves and keep trying. Imagine if teachers had a cheering section, much like they are for their students, to keep things good and positive.

 Listening to our own voice, remembering our own advice, especially when things get tough, can make a significant difference.

TAKING YOUR OWN ADVICE

Everyone can learn from the positive support of teachers, even themselves. For Example: *"Do your best."* It's said to set expectations, to encourage quality, and to support the variety of skill levels in a classroom. But, even more importantly it comes from truth. We can't do more.

Teachers often feel like they have the weight of the world on their shoulders. There's never enough time (or energy) to get it all done. However, how good would it feel to know that what we are giving is enough. If we could step back and hear *"Just do your best"* - maybe we could understand that our best is not only good enough - it's all that we can expect from ourselves.

"Keep trying."

When the weight of the day is getting you down, when we can't quite reach that one student, or the workload seems stacked too high, wouldn't it be nice to have someone to remind us to keep moving forward?

Teachers have a great way of nudging students along when they feel stuck or burned out on a particular task or skill. They are wonderful motivators because they need to engage all students. So, when the teacher is feeling stuck or burned out - remember your own advice - *"just keep trying"*. Sure once you get over this hump, they'll be another one - but that's life, filled with lots of tries.

"You can do it."

Whether you are a first-year teacher or a veteran administrator, everyone could use to hear these four little words now and again. The field of education can be highly demanding. It can be physically and emotionally taxing. There is often a lack of vulnerability in education (like many professions). When things get tough, the general unspoken rule is to suck it up and act like a professional. But, what if we could say to one another - "wow that was a tough day" or "I'm having a hard time" without fear or judgment? What if we could hear our own words as an educator echo back to us *"You can do", "You've got this"*? A little acknowledgment and encouragement will go a long way in building strength and resilience. After all, that's why we say it to our students.

"Tomorrow is a new day."

Imagine if no matter how the day presented itself, how tired or stressed we felt at the end of the day of teaching, that our last thoughts leaving the classroom room were of hope. Often they are, but I know I have been stuck in the funk too many times where I am watching the clock ready to race out of the room away from the day - only to end my evening wide awake in bed replaying every interaction and decision I made.

When teachers tell their students that *"tomorrow is another day"* they are giving them permission to accept what happened today, but let it go - because there is hope. There are limitless opportunities and many more chances to get things right. If we left our classrooms with that insight, we would sleep better, and we could start each day with a renewed optimism for the potential presented to us.

So please, for today accept and believe these words. *"Just do your best and keep trying because you can do it and tomorrow is a new day"*

SELF-EFFICACY IN TEACHING

Educators need to believe in their own abilities. They need to feel empowered by the tools, skills, and resources available to them. They need to know that they can move the needle forward and facilitate change. After all, that is why most of us entered the field, to make a difference. Therefore, a boost in self-efficacy is a boost in resilience.

Teacher self-efficacy is a teacher's belief in their own ability to positively impact their students' lives. When educators become overwhelmed with new initiatives, mounting workloads, and challenging student behaviors their view of themselves can alter. Teachers question their capabilities as change-agents within their students' lives, and the process begins to snowball. The more teachers become overwhelmed, the more their self-efficacy dips, and the less they make a difference. This process can play on repeat indefinitely, eventually leading to burnout.

The good news is the opposite is also true. When teachers believe they have the skills needed to deal with challenging student behavior and heavy workloads they feel less burnout.[35] Confidence is deeply embedded in their capacity to teach and ability to take risks.[50] Of course, this isn't news to classroom teachers who work each day to build their students' confidence with the understanding that when they believe they can do it, they will. It's just more difficult sometimes to do that for ourselves.

Self-efficacy is a powerful piece of teacher resilience. It goes far beyond self-esteem and even personal burnout. A teacher who exhibits high self-efficacy, meaning they know they can effect change within their position, is more likely to have students who achieve and is more likely to stay in teaching.[8] This knowledge is powerful when applied to discussions on keeping good, qualified teachers in the classroom.

The benefits of fostering high teacher self-efficacy reach far beyond the teachers; it impacts student success and the teaching profession as a whole.

 The more teachers believe they can create change, the more they can.

Self-efficacy is an essential piece in the framework of fighting burnout and reclaiming the joy in teaching. It is both a mindset and a tangible set of tools. It is believing in your abilities as an educator and knowing you have the support of the people in your system to make decisions and create positive change.

OWN YOUR TEACHING

Resilience theory, at its core, is about the strength to thrive in the face of adversity.[40] This takes work, practice and an understanding of our limitations.

We all would like to think that we can do it all, that we can be dynamic educators who connect with all of our students while creating meaningful relationships with our colleagues and maintaining a fulfilling and active social life outside of school. However, the reality is that being an educator means we are in a constant tug-of-war for our time and energy. This struggle leads to guilt and stress and an overwhelming feeling that whatever we do is never enough.

Educators who stretch themselves too thin often have lost sight of their needs and limitations of time and energy. When we don't extend the caring and compassion that we exert to our students back to ourselves, when our need to help others overtakes our need for self-care, we become overwhelmed and drained. Burnout is a syndrome of emotional exhaustion that can cause educators to distance themselves from those around them and feel less accomplished.[42] And, students know this. They recognize it when a teacher is fledging, which means it impacts our ability to teach.

However, educators are not helpless, quite the opposite. Reframing our compassion to care without burnout out makes us more effective teachers.[50] It's about healthful limits and self-awareness, both skills which can be taught, learned, and practiced.

 By creating boundaries we are better educators because we are taking ownership of our purpose.

We demonstrate our healthful limits when we step into school with the intention of being present and the belief we can make a change, knowing that we have mapped a path to resilience and left time for ourselves.

Owning our teaching means taking hold of our resilience, knowing when to give to others and when to give to ourselves. **Self-care is not selfish.** And when you take time for yourself, to reflect and refresh, you have more to give later on.

There are added benefits to owning your teaching. When teachers understand resilience skills, they can pass them on and promote them in their school and to their students.[50] This connection means that not only are the teachers benefiting from learning resilience strategies and protective practices, but the students and staff are as well.

 When we invest in teacher resilience we invest in the success of our schools.

Connecting with your sense of purpose, listening to your advice, owning your teaching, and believing you can make a difference are significant factors in teacher resilience.[17] As educators, we develop a certain level of patience. We don't expect students to master tasks and balance everything perfectly right away. We are there to nurture and support them as they develop skills and find their path. It's time we, as educators, grant ourselves the same patience we extend to our students. Building resilience is a process, and remember, it takes work. It takes work to implement new strategies and approaches. It takes reflection – on your purpose and practices. And, it takes change – to live what you teach.

Discussion Questions

1. How can we, as educators, empower ourselves to listen to our own voice? What reminders might we need?

2. When you reflect on your self-efficacy as a teacher/leader do you see yourself as someone who has the power and support to facilitate change? How so?

3. How can teacher self-efficacy be supported and heightened in your school?

4. Where (or when) in your day-to-day teaching practice do you see a need to create defined boundaries? Think time and space.

*C*hapter *11*

Reclaim the Joy

*C*hapter *Overview*

- Examine your current habits.

- Learn what is needed to make a meaningful mindset shift.

- Understand the difference in responses between a resilient and non-resilient educator.

- Discover the power of taking action toward your own joy.

Reclaiming the Joy in Teaching requires action – this goes beyond understanding what is within and outside of our control and deeper than making time for ourselves. It involves an examination of our habits, a shift in mindset, and a plan of action. We must consciously move forward toward joy while learning to side-step the common pitfalls of occupational stress and burnout.

EXAMINING YOUR CURRENT HABITS

So far in this book, we have taken steps to explore where you are in your career using reflections, self-inventories, and discussion questions. If you are following along in *The Definitive Joy in Teaching Workbook*, then you have completed numerous activities to evaluate your current state within the education profession. But, how did you get where you are?

Understanding what practices and circumstances played a role in your current level of occupational enjoyment is the next step. It is crucial to realize that, no matter whether you are the happiest you have ever been or you are teetering on the edge of burnout, certain pieces have fallen into place to cause your current state.

 With a reexamination of habits, a strong mindset, and the resiliency tools to inspire action teachers can reconnect with their purpose.

Take a moment to reflect on your current practices. What are your obstacles that stand in the way of thoroughly enjoying being an educator? Is it lack of autonomy or recognition? Student behavior? Class schedule?... as we know, the list goes on.

Now consider how you respond to these obstacles. Make a list. If you experience a lack of autonomy, do you use department meeting time to complain about your curricular woes? If you feel a lack of recognition, do you shut down at staff meetings feeling unseen and unheard? If you have student behavior issues, do you tackle them with the same strategies and consequences? If your daily schedule is a cause of stress, do you come to work earlier or stay later to deal with the lack of time during your scheduled hours. How you respond to your obstacles has a lot to do with your current feelings toward the education profession. Consider what you do or have done to facilitate change. And, if you haven't tried to change things, ask yourself, why?

Finally, evaluate your response – it reveals more than just how you handle the stressors you face each day. How we respond to the obstacles that stand between ourselves and our happiness and a sense of purpose speaks volumes about our mindset as educators.

SHIFTING YOUR MINDSET

So, l let's talk mindset. There are many educational books and resources that point to mindset as being a significant factor in professional effectiveness and success. There are school-wide initiatives based on shifting the mindsets of students. The one perhaps most people are aware of is Growth Mindset, so let's start there.

The concept of growth mindset is attributed, originally, to Dr. Carol Dweck who asserts that a growth mindset, as opposed to a fixed mindset, encourages effort and persistence through obstacles.[51] It encourages those who adopt the mindset to be inspired by criticism and embrace challenges. All of these are good qualities to implement at school and in life – I don't believe anyone would dispute this.

For those of you who are unfamiliar with the topic, growth mindset is merely a way of looking at tasks, abilities, and achievements as ongoing developments rather than destinations. It has changed the way teachers and employers respond and praise, and it is touted as a path to higher levels of achievement.[52] For example, instead of saying, "You did awesome," instead you would say, "You're on the right track," The idea being – it's all a journey and you can always improve. Growth mindset has also inspired a new approach to self-talk. Instead of saying, "I'm not

117

good at this," you could say "What am I missing?" or "What other strategies can I use to do better?"

Growth mindset, for all its buzz, is optimism powered by affirmation. Without setting a course of action, these affirmations cannot take shape.

 Many educators are missing an essential piece of the mindset shift. Action.

Whether the audience is students, teachers, or employees, without providing them the tools to place their growth mindset into action, it becomes nothing but happy noise.

I, myself have sat in meetings where I have both been taught how to create a growth mindset for myself and presented the importance of it for my students. I have talked with numerous teachers who have sat through the same. No one can disagree with the positive perspective of a growth mindset, and I am not suggesting that we should. However, the piece that is so important is almost always missing. We have to prepare teachers and students to take action when it comes to facing obstacles.

 We have to provide the necessary tools and techniques to exert the extra effort that the growth mindset encourages.

The Teacher Mindset

There are those who will take the initiative on their own. Those who will learn about growth mindset and implement it flawlessly and allow the renewed perspective to help launch them to higher levels of achievement – blasting past obstacles and boosting up from criticism. However, just to play devil's advocate - is this the person who a growth mindset really can help the most? The person who is already a self-starter, a go-getter, and who will use the tools provided without further instruction?

Probably not.

We all know the teacher in the staff meeting who is a bit of a downer. Or, the one with running total of the number of days left of the school year tallied from day one. We know the teacher who is convinced the school, students and staff included, is a non-effective mess. They don't offer solutions, but aren't afraid to vocalize their dissatisfaction. Perhaps, in some ways, you can relate yourself.

This is the teacher who needs growth mindset the most. But, is this the teacher who when given the information and spiel on growth mindset will take it and just run with it – turn everything around and be a positive leader for the school?

It is very unlikely.

That is because, this teacher, who is crying out for a shift in mindset (whether consciously or not), has developed a habit of negativity. This educator is going to understand the concept of a growth mindset, but may not have the tools and/or motivation to change things around for them self.

When you review your list of obstacles standing between you and your joy in teaching and when you reflect on your responses to those obstacles, are you exhibiting a growth mindset?

Are you prepared to take action?

In order for our obstacles to be overcome, especially the ones that are not within our control, we need to consider a new approach.

Without building strong resilience, growth mindset stays in our minds. We need action.

This is why resilience training is so important. Teaching teachers how to build resiliency provides them a platform to take action. By giving teachers the tools to move forward they are able to disrupt previous habits of negativity or inaction and take steps toward becoming a stronger educator.

TAKING ACTION TO RECLAIM YOUR JOY

Burnout can impact the intrinsic motivation of educators.[42] It can cause them to lose their enthusiasm and career idealism which can lead to discouragement. Without action, occupational stress leads to a slippery slope of dissatisfaction, loss of purpose and eventual burnout.

Just knowing that you can take action can make a difference in teacher stress. Hope for the future is a common trait in teacher resilience building.[41] Recognizing which habits are counterproductive to happiness and job satisfaction and shifting our mindset to focus on the positive, positions us, as educators, to take action. When teachers don't see where they can effect change or better their situation they lose hope and burnout begins to creep in. Once teachers reach burnout stage, it becomes more difficult to recognize paths toward resilience and change.

 It is cyclical. Lack of ability to take action can lead to burnout and burnout leads to a lack of ability to take action.

Burnout

Lack of ability to take

Action

A resilient educator will still have bad days and may disengage at times. However, they will always re-engage, ready to try a new approach.[41] They know they have the ability to change their situation, to better their days and their students'. Instead of blaming the circumstance, which we discovered way back in Chapter One are very often out of our control as educators, a resilient teacher searches for a new path to joy.

A non-resilient teacher asks, *Why did this situation happen to me?*

A resilient teacher asks, *What new approach can I bring to this situation?*

The Skills You Have And The Skills You Need

Confronting problems, making decisions, and developing the skills to handle difficult situations starts the moment an educator steps in the classroom. These skills are directly transferable to resilience.

Each day teachers are developing the characteristics to be resilient - you just may not recognize it.

Resilience is a matter of using the skills you have, coupled with the tools and techniques necessary to face challenges and overcome obstacles. Creating an action plan is an excellent method to remind yourself of the paths in front of you that you can take to reclaim your joy in teaching. You can create your own or use the template in *The Definitive Joy in Teaching Workbook*.

RESILIENCE TRAINING

Chapters Thirteen and Fourteen provide many of the necessary tools and techniques that you can apply to build resilience and fight burnout. Finding which of these work for you is how you will build your framework for action. But, innately knowing that you can take action is an essential first piece that must be in place. It can be difficult to pull yourself up when you are down. Relying on your support network (both in and out of school) can motivate teachers who need a boost. An understanding that everyone has something they can identify to work on and that resilience is a process are all factors in committing to a resilient approach.

The entire ecosystem of a school (or district) can be impacted by simply giving teachers a voice, providing them the knowledge and tools to develop resiliency in their careers. Consistent professional development, not just a one-time mention in passing, offers teachers an opportunity to rewrite their story and reframe their perspective toward becoming a more resilient educator. Remember time, space, and motivation – these are the ingredients for a successful resilience program. And, they are what you need to reclaim your joy in teaching.

Teacher Resilience Education is training focused on giving teachers the tools to get the most joy out of their careers. It offers research-based actionable steps toward reducing occupational stress. Resiliency education puts applicable tools in the hands of teachers so that they can take on the increasing stress of a career in education. For what resilience training can look like visit **www.joyinteaching.com/offerings**.

 Resilience and teacher well-being need to be included in the everyday language of your school and deserve a seat at the professional development table.

Teacher Resilience Education treats educators like professionals and gives them the tools to reclaim the joy in teaching.[53] When the well-being of teachers is a purposeful piece of professional development, the whole school wins. Teacher resilience means teachers have a depth of resources they can pull from to adapt to stressful situations (which we all know are in no shortage within the field of education). Teachers are able to persevere, have a sense of control when things get messy, and can view themselves and their position with a sense of optimism and strength.

Discussion Questions

1. How can identifying our current habits and our compulsory responses move us forward?

2. What obstacle can you share with others to help hold yourself accountable to make a change?

3. How can colleagues support a mass mindset shift toward action when it comes to building resilience and reclaiming their joy in teaching?

4. How is teacher resilience represented in professional development at your school? Where are opportunities for dialogue?

*C*hapter *12*

Save the Teachers

*C*hapter *Overview*

- Review the rewards and heartbreak of caring deeply

- Understand that resilience is a learned skill.

- Discover how empowering teachers with resiliency tools reverses the negative spiral of teacher stress.

- Learn how building resilience positions you as a disruptor in the field of education.

You may not have control over all the factors within teaching that cause you stress. You probably cannot, at least immediately, effect change in ways that will drastically alter the conditions in which you work (that doesn't mean it's not worth trying though). What you do have absolute power over is how you react to your stressors. What you give your energy to, and how you choose to respond is 100% connected to how you experience your career in education. You are in the power position when it comes to reclaiming your joy in teaching – even on days when it doesn't seem that way at all.

WHY TEACHING IS THE BEST (AND THE WORST) JOB EVER

As an educator, whether that be teacher, administrator, coach, or aide, you get to be a part of your students' stories, share in their successes and lead them toward greatness. You see how much your belief in them can change how they see themselves, and on a regular basis you get to have some very funny and interesting conversations with young people.

And those young people, the kids, our students - well, they are the best (and the worst).[54] Yes, I said it. We want to see them succeed on a level deeper than just because it is our job. We lose sleep over them, worry about their well-being and wonder what they are up to when they aren't at school. We believe in them when they don't believe in themselves. And there is not much that feels as warm and good as helping a student achieve what they thought was impossible.

We love them like our own because they are our kids But, they are kids and eventually, if you teach long enough you are going to get your heartbroken. When that kid who you stay late after school with each day to work on homework, that kid who you sneak a granola bar to each morning because he's hungry, that kid who told you all his personal baggage and you have sympathized with and supported every way you can does something undermining or disrespectful, when he falls off the path you have created – it hurts. It feels personal. And you have to let it feel personal, knowing that he's just a kid and he still needs you and your support – maybe even more now.

126

It's the nature of teaching, the heart-wrenching truth of teaching, that when you care deeply about your students, you open yourself up to some pain.

The key is to not let it close you off and to move forward knowing you can and do make a positive impact in ways both seen and unseen ways.

So, what do we do?

Maximize the good, because it is really good. Celebrate the accomplishments, big and small. Remind ourselves that we can never see the full impact of what we do each day and believe that we are making a positive difference.

Minimize the bad, because it has the potential to be really bad. Cut yourself some slack. Know that each day offers new opportunities to reteach and rebuild. Take care of yourself – you are doing more good than you even know and you are no good at all to your students if you let yourself burn out. Taking steps to build your resilience and strengthen your approach to the occupational stressors is yes, good for you, but it also is what your students need you to do.

In the end, we take the good with the bad, because we believe in what we do and we know that we can make a difference, even on the days we don't see it.

TEACHER RESILIENCE AS PRIORITY

In Part One of this book set the stage as we departed on our journey toward resilience. We know from Chapter One that reflection is critical place to beginning on the path toward stronger resilience. The self-inventory led you through a process of analyzing what is and is not within your control when it comes to occupational stress. Chapter Two connected research on teacher-well-being to demonstrate how interwoven the stress of educators is to the success of their students and schools. Chapter

Three laid out the severity of burnout and many of the common related symptoms.

Part Two of this book paved the road of resilience by showcasing some of the necessary pieces that support a resilient approach to education. In Chapter Four, it was demonstrated how meaningful it is to connect to your purpose and remembering why you started in the first place is still an integral part of who you are as an educator. Chapter Five delved into how a supportive community and network can be an essential piece of your resilience. And then, Chapter Six highlighted how creating an intentional culture of recognition and respect can bolster individual and shared morale within a school.

In Part Three of this book, we traveled the road to resilience while developing an understanding of some of the actions available to take control of your resiliency. We understand from Chapter Seven that infusing play, innovation, exploration, and fun into your classroom can benefit both the teacher and students. Chapter Eight showed how opening up and sharing about yourself and your interests can become a resilience-building strategy. In Chapter Nine, you were provided many timesaving tips so that you can focus what matters most within the hectic school day. Also, you were encouraged to consider your strengths as an educator and how to leverage them as a way of building resilience.

In Part Four of this book we see that the journey is the destination by examining our role and how we can create change. In Chapter Ten you were encouraged to see how taking your own advice as an educator can be empowering. Chapter Eleven encouraged you to take action against occupational stress and burnout. And then in this chapter, Chapter Twelve, you are shown how you can become a disruptor in the field, changing the current trend of burnout.

Lastly, in Part Five of this book, you will find tangible steps to take action against some of the common occupational stressors associated with a career in education. If you are following along in *The Definitive Joy in Teaching Workbook,* you will have workshopped many of these ideas and developed a clear framework to move forward. Chapter Thirteen offers a list of resilience building strategies that you can use to transform your day and start anew tomorrow. Chapter Fourteen provides a list of protective practices that you can adopt as part of your approach to your career and your life. The key is to try new ideas, take on new methods to combat the occupational stress and burnout that for far too long have been synonymous with the life of an educator.

Resilience is a Skill

It is possible to turn back the clock of stress and burnout. It is possible to reconnect with your purpose as an educator. And, it is possible is reclaim your joy in teaching.

Maybe you are in a school that has made a conscious decision to support teacher well-being through resilience training. Maybe not. Either way, the best course of action is developing a personalized framework for action filled with strategies that work for you.

 Teacher resilience is a learned skill - and not one often addressed in teacher education.

Eliminating all the sources of stress within the education field is not possible. Like with any career and perhaps more than most, a career in education offers many rewarding moments, but between those moments it is demanding, fast-paced, and unpredictable.[53] Teaching is one of the most fulfilling careers there are, but it also has the reputation of taking a serious toll on those who have dedicated their lives to it.

Focusing on teacher resilience gives back to those who have given so much and allows them and our schools to be the best they can be. To do this – to learn the skill of resilience – we need to go back to where we began, to reexamine the impact of teacher well-being and how resiliency can facilitate change.

YOU AS A DISRUPTOR

In Chapter Two, I presented the image of a downward spiral based on the initial research that motivated me to write this book. The spiral demonstrated the depth of impact on teacher well-being. It showcased that as teacher well-being plummets, it takes with it the effectiveness of our schools. It illustrated that stressed teachers equal stressed students and that in turn negatively influences student success. It painted a picture of the negative impact that disregarding teacher resilience creates.

Well, what if I told you we just reversed the spiral?

That by going through this book and applying the tools and techniques to build resilience, fight burnout, and reclaim the joy in teaching you have in fact altered the state of things. You have become a disruptor.

Take a look:

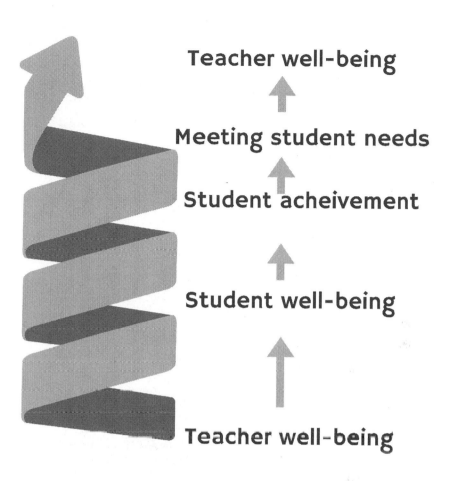

Teacher well-being

↑

Meeting student needs

↑

Student acheivement

↑

Student well-being

↑

Teacher well-being

You see? It remains true that teacher well-being has the power to impact student and school success, but now it is reversed.

What This Means For You

We know that teachers have the power to raise student stress levels merely by bringing their high levels of occupational stress into the classroom. We understand that teacher stress equals student stress. But, just knowing that a teacher's well-being has the power to impact the well-being of students is motivation to develop a resilient approach to education.

We also know that a student's well-being directly connects to their academic success. This connection is why we build relationships, sneak hungry kids food, bring in extra supplies, and lay awake worrying – we know that there is a level of well-being that needs to be satisfied before a student can be expected to focus on school matters. This was as true in the 1940's with Maslow's Hierarchy of Needs[55] as it is now with the ACES (adverse childhood experiences) initiatives.[56] Student well-being is vital to their success, and teachers play a part in this.

 Teacher resilience positively impacts students.

It's that simple. Educators who believe they can effect change and can handle the occupational stress that teaching can throw at them positively influence their students' well-being, which in turn positively influences the students' achievement, which results in positively influencing the students' needs and how we address them. And, when you have a school on this upward spiral – it keeps spiraling.

The more a staff taps into resiliency and fosters support for teacher well-being, the more the teachers, the students, and the school as a whole benefit. When the community is supportive, positive teacher retention rises.[57] Do you see yet how becoming a resilient educator positions you as a disruptor in the profession?

By reclaiming the joy in teaching and supporting those around you to do the same, you are flipping the script on the current statistics of teacher burnout and the looming teacher shortage. When teachers are resilient, they have the tools to deal with the obstacles they face and the techniques to handle occupational stress in ways that do not impact their performance. They know there are actions they can take to thwart burnout and overcome negativity. They have the confidence in themselves to know that when things get tough, they have the ability to bounce back. Staring down burnout, ready to take action allows you to, in effect, change the course of history.

A school that has invested in teacher resilience and placed importance on the well-being of its staff has invested in the success of its students. Educators equipped with resilience building strategies, clear on their purpose, and filled with hope for the potential of their school year will thrive in the face of adversity and defy the odds. A staff that supports one another's resilience creates a better, stronger school. And, an educator that seeks new ways to handle occupational stress and burnout while not giving up on why they entered the profession can and will reclaim their joy in teaching.

Discussion Questions

1. How does your resilience positively impact your students?

2. How do you envision the power of teacher resilience's ability to impact your school?

3. In what ways will you make teacher resilience a priority?

Part 5

Packing and Unpacking

*C*hapter *13*

Resilience Strategies for Educators

*C*hapter *O*verview

* Learn about what makes a resilience strategy.

* Review a variety of resilience strategies and how they can relieve the stress associated with a career in education.

* Consider what resilience strategies would be beneficial to your framework of action.

They say do what you love, and you'll never work a day in your life because it won't feel like work. Well, some days teaching is going to feel like work, but it's all worth it when you know your purpose, you are clear on your passion, and you possess the tools to fight burnout and reclaim your joy in teaching.

It is time to build your framework, to create your path to joy. You understand what is at stake and how stress and burnout impacts you and all those around you. You see the power of taking action. And, you want to move forward.

WHAT ARE RESILIENCE STRATEGIES

Different authors and experts have varying views of how to define resilience strategies vs. protective practices. For our purposes in this book we are dividing resilience strategies as tangible, often quick, actions you can take to provide yourself a boost. These strategies alleviate the impact occupational stress – often temporarily. Protective practices, featured in Chapter Fourteen, are actions you can embed into your routine. These practices can become habits that create long-term changes in how you relate and react to the occupational stress. Sure, there is some overlap between the categories of resilience strategies and protective practices; a combination of both will fuel your framework of action and provide you the best defense against teacher burnout.

As you go through the lists (in this chapter and the next), you may realize that some of the skills you read about you already possess. Some of the basic building blocks of resiliency align with the necessary skills of being an educator. These already exist inside you – learning from previous experiences, problem-solving skills, leaning on your support network.[15,58] Do not discount these. Skills that you are already familiar with, strategies you already employ, should stand as a foundation to your framework for action. You can lean on the tools and techniques that you already use, whether you previously recognized resiliency skills or not.

If you are following along in *The Definitive Joy in Teaching Workbook,* you will find the same list as is below along with room to make notes, rank, and add ideas. When strategies have been discussed previously in this book, you will find a chapter notation.

138

RESILIENCE STRATEGIES
> ## ➤ USE YOUR SENSES

A lot falls into this category. Consider how all of your senses can provide a sense of calm and re-centering. The feel of grass or sand between your toes, the sound of crashing waves or trickling water, the dynamic colors of a setting sun. Taking notice of the little things, yes, even in the school day, can be a satisfying way of de-stressing, even if just for a moment.

Music

The type of music that is playing in the classroom impacts the learning and behaviors in the classroom.[59] Music can provide a sense of calm or enliven a lesson. Use it to your advantage to enhance the mood of your classes and your day.

Light

Some classrooms don't have windows (I've been there), and some have windows that won't open (been there too), but do what you can to open the classroom up. Maybe that's fully opening a window to let in the fresh air and sunlight, maybe that's just opening the blinds. Give everyone's eyes a break from the fluorescent lights.

Scent

You could bring fresh flowers, a candle (if permitted), or an essential oil diffuser. A calming scent like lavender can infuse a sense of calm into the room while masking odors that are less kind to our noses.

Fidgets

I know there are some definite feelings about fidgets – you know, the little toys to keep little hands busy. These are great for some students who need a little help focusing or need to satisfy a sensory need during learning time, but have you ever tried them?

You may find them surprisingly relaxing and easy to sneak into your hand during a stressful day.

➤ **METHODS & APPROACHES** (Ch. 7)

Beyond breaking your routine, consider how what you teach can be introduced in new ways to boost both yours and your students' excitement. An approach to teaching that connects activities to real-world experiences promotes self-efficacy and boosts interest, motivation, and engagement in the classroom.

Innovation

This approach values students' ideas and gives them an opportunity to take ownership of their learning.

Exploration

An emphasis on exploring encourages students to seek the potential of their ideas and learn from their mistakes.

Play

This is naturally linked to children already and provides students opportunity to earn and grow through social interaction.

Fun

In the classroom, fun boosts interest and engagement and encourages students' desire to learn.

Creativity

Infusing creative moments into your school day can become a defining piece of your classroom culture through building a supportive community that honors individual ideas.

➤ **BRING IN YOUR INTERESTS** (Ch.8)

By bringing your interests into your classroom, you are giving your students a way of connecting with you. Whether your interests are similar to theirs or seen as goofy or outdated, showing that you are more than just academics humanizes you for your students and allows you to merge your passions.

➤ **PROTECT YOUR TIME** (Ch. 9)

Say "No"

Choose the most meaningful and necessary tasks and say "No" say "No" to the rest (when you can).

Say "Yes"

Listen to your intuition, and give to yourself and your well-being.

No more teacher guilt

Give yourself permission to take care of yourself.

Set up systems

Encourage student autonomy and organize your classroom to work more efficiently.

Practice being present

Reduce multi-tasking and focus on one task at a time.

Pick and choose your extracurriculars

Choose activities that are the best use of your time and the most meaningful.

Formative over Summative

When possible, assess without the test and use formative assessments to gauge student learning.

Streamline your schoolbag

Only bring home what you plan to and have time to work on, leave the rest at school.

Batch your work

Approach your work in like-segments to work through tasks with the greatest productivity.

➤ **WRITE IT DOWN**

Writing out the happenings of your day gets it out of your head.[60] Having a place to express your thoughts means that they aren't still in the back of your mind when you leave school and they aren't swirling around when you are trying to sleep.

➢ PLAN INTO THE FUTURE

Take a look at your calendar; find something to look forward to. If there isn't anything in the near future (say within a month), then schedule something. Maybe it's a weekend getaway, a birthday or anniversary celebration, a night out with friends – whatever it is, plot it out, plan for it, and give yourself something that will keep you moving forward.

➢ TREAT YOURSELF

Giving back to yourself can provide you the little boost you need to reenter your classroom with a brighter outlook. It doesn't have to be a whole day, but take a little break and give to yourself. You won't regret it. Even on a teacher's salary, it's possible to find a way to do something special just for you.

➢ ORGANIZE YOUR SPACE

For many people, an organized space provides mental clarity too. When your surroundings are in order, it is less taxing on you psychologically and allows you to have the mental fortitude to focus on what is most important. So, organize that desk and stack those papers, it can help you.

➢ BREAK ROUTINE

Think back to your student days. What do you remember most? It's probably not the days that all felt the same. The days that will be most memorable to your students are the days something special happens. So, introduce some novelty, initiate a new activity or project, break up the routine – it could become the best thing you do for you and your students.

➢ BUDDY UP

It's time to make a conscious decision about how you spend your time and energy. Consider those you work with and who you can turn to when you need a quick jolt of encouragement. Buddy up with the people who can make you the best teacher you can be, and the best version of yourself possible.

➤ **MINI-BREAKS**

Schedule a few moments in your day. Maybe a few minutes before the students come in the room, or before you head down to the teachers' lounge for lunch. Consciously planning small moments will give you time to recharge before facing the rest of what the day has in store. Adding mini-breaks into your day ahead of time holds you accountable for taking them later.

➤ **DESIGN YOUR SPACE**

The Reggio Emilia approach considers the classroom the "third teacher.[61] It becomes a flexible space wherein the teacher and student learn together. However, most classrooms are institutional in their aesthetic.[62] Manilla. Plain. Consider ways to update your space.

Add some green

Count yourself lucky if your school is in a safe neighborhood and has an outdoor classroom or learning area. And, utilize it as much as possible. If not, adopt some houseplants. It will improve the décor and provide a little sense of the outdoors inside.

Move in

Okay don't completely move in, but don't be afraid to personalize your space. Hang some pictures of your family or pets, add some items that make you feel comfortable.

➤ **RANDOM ACTS OF KINDNESS**

Positivity boosts positivity. The more positivity you are around, the more positive you become. So, think about who you engage with and who engages with you during the day, because it works the same way with negativity. Are you giving and getting the encouragement you need? Consider how you can unexpectedly brighten a colleague's day.

➤ **GOALS**

Set goals for yourself. Break down long -term goals into smaller and quicker attainable pieces. Write them down. Make lists and keep them near. It feels good to cross off accomplishments and see that you are moving forward.

➢ CLASSROOM MINDFULNESS

A full day of being "on" can take its toll on everyone. Think of your students – they move from one subject to the next and are expected to be switching modes constantly while adhering to expectations and doing their best. Students can benefit from a moment of calm in their day too – so take them along with you. Infuse some mindfulness and/or meditative practices in your classroom and find calm together.

Discussion Questions

1. What resilience strategies do you already use? How can you lean on these as strengths in your framework of action?
2. What resilience strategies stand out to you as necessary in your approach to education?
3. What resilience strategies could your school adopt as a mission or group initiative to bolster staff strength?

*C*hapter *14*

Protective Practices for Educators

*C*hapter *O*verview

- Learn how a protective practice differs from a resilience strategy.

- Review a variety of protective practices and how they can become a buffer between you and the occupational stress in education.

- Consider what protective practices would be beneficial to your framework of action.

You often hear the term protective practices (or protective factors) in relation to conditions that advance child welfare. However, as we look at ways of advancing teacher well-being we see a need for practices that can serve as a buffer between educators and the occupational stressors they may face. Protective practices, for our purposes, are those practices that with some time can become habits that stand in the way of stress impacting the well-being of teachers.

Protective practices and resilience strategies are both actionable ways of dealing with stress. They both deserve space in your action plan, but they are not the same. While many resilience strategies have the power to give educators a boost right now, protective practices can offer more long-term solutions to occupational stress and burnout.[63] It can take some trial and error to find which protective practices work for you and your routines. Some need a controlled environment or a time set aside. Just as in Chapter Thirteen, if you are following along in *The Definitive Joy in Teaching Workbook* you will see all of the following protective practices along with space to reflect and make notes.

PROTECTIVE PRACTICES

➢ DEEP BREATHING

You can do this in the classroom or hallway, even when surrounded by students. At first notice of those uneasy feelings, inhale long and slow and exhale even slower. Do this 8-10 times and feel the tension begin to release. Make a habit of doing this often. Deep breathing can help reset your stress-level and allow you to face new challenges with a more resilient perspective.

➢ SELF-TALK

Self-talk refers to your inner dialog - the little voice in your head that encourages you most of the time, but sometimes gets negative. When your self-talk begins to be counter-productive, take note. This often is reflective of what is going on in your world. Consciously, change the voice. When negative thoughts creep in, and they will, turn your thoughts toward the positive. Look to what you can change and remember your mindset.

➤ PROGRESSIVE MUSCLE RELAXATION

Often paired with meditation, progressive muscle relaxation is the tightening and relaxing of each muscle group to gain awareness of tensions. You can start with your toes and work your way up – recognizing which areas are carrying tension and letting go of stress as you move through your body. This can be done sitting at your desk – no ohms, no chanting – just a quick moment to relax and reset.

➤ REFLECTION

This could easily be tied in with journaling and several other resilience strategies, but deserves its own focus as well. By taking time to reflect on your day, the activities that went well, and the ones that didn't, you are acknowledging them to release them. When reflection becomes part of your daily routine, whether it is in a journal, blog, or nightly discussion with your partner, you can let go, so that you are not lying away at night still running through the day. Consider what you are grateful for in each day to help remind yourself to not dwell on the negative.

➤ YOGA

Explore mindfulness within yoga. Stretch your body and quiet the mind. Many teachers have incorporated yoga into their classes as a brain break for both them and their students. Yoga could easily be placed in Chapter Thirteen as a resilience strategy, but for those who have made yoga a part of their routine it becomes more than just a stretch. Yoga can be a means of daily renewal.

➤ MEDITATION

Meditation can look many different ways, but it all equates to quieting and slowing down, focusing on breathing and giving yourself a moment of peace. Some teachers find meditation to be a great way to start their prep time, while others have incorporated it into their mindfulness practices with their students.

➤ VISUALIZATIONS

Picture peaceful, calm situations, use your senses to focus on the positive, change your screen saver, post some signs – all these can aid in taking your mind to a calm place through visualization. The key is to have a picture in mind that you can conjure up that soothes you; some people have a go-to serene scene they picture, others use a mantra to cue relaxing images. You can start by brainstorming places you have been where you have felt refreshed and calm.

➤ AVOIDANCE OF STRESS DRIVERS

You can't avoid many of your occupational stressors. We have established that. But, consider what you can actively avoid. Social media and the 24-hour news cycle are both triggers for stress, especially when the news directly relates to education. Turning off your TV or avoiding social media for a while doesn't make you much less informed, you can still advocate for your students without constantly being bombarded by bad news. The same goes for toxic areas at work. If you know that the teacher's lounge or the south hallway is an area where teachers congregate for negativity or gossip, you can choose not to engage, you are still part of the community, but you are protecting yourself as well. Think about what areas of stress you can take action to avoid, or even experience less, in your daily routine.

➤ RELY ON YOUR STRENGTHS (Ch. 9)

In Chapter Nine, we went into detail of the strengths that can benefit you as a teacher. By being an aware and reflective educator, you can understand what your strengths are and how to use them to help deal with challenges that may arise.

➤ HEALTHFUL LIFESTYLE

Your lifestyle can support your resilience. Clean living - regular exercise, going outdoors, eating nourishing food, and positive social connections, all prepare you to be your best when dealing with challenging situations within education. When you feel strong and clear-headed, you can make decisions easier and tackle what is ahead with confidence.

> **PURPOSE** (Ch. 4)

Educators who have a strong sense of purpose can handle difficult situations and the subsequent occupational stress with confidence because they have an underlying strength driving them. Leading with purpose means that the "WHY" is stronger than most challenges a career in education can throw at you. When you can keep this in the forefront of your mind, be it making a difference in the world, helping students realize their potential, building stronger communities…, you approach obstacles with clarity. The daily challenges begin to shrink in comparison to your lofty purpose, and you can deal with stressors with tenacity.

> **SUPPORT SYSTEM** (Ch. 5)

Whether you garner support from your connections in school, at home, within your faith, or elsewhere, having a support system in place is extremely effective in buffering the stress that can accumulate from a career in education. Your support system can be one person or fifty, either way, it provides you an outlet, someone who will listen, work through issues, and help you get out of your head.

> **CLEAR BOUNDARIES**

Defining boundaries in education can be difficult. You want to be "all in" for your students, and you are, but that doesn't mean that you don't need some time and space to yourself. Consciously defining your boundaries and sticking to them gives you security in knowing that there WILL be decompression time. Maybe you start setting the alarm on your phone for when you will definitely leave school, or you state that students will no longer be in the room during your lunchtime, or planning time, whatever boundaries you set, do them thoughtfully and then abide by your definitions.

> ➤ **CONTENT KNOWLEDGE**

Maybe you haven't ever considered content knowledge as a tool in your pocket when it comes to protecting yourself against the stress of a career in education. The truth is, your understanding of the pedagogy behind what you do can be a significant player in your defense against occupational stress. By staying up-to-date on what is happening within your discipline and what is going on within the field of education, you can face challenges with confidence. Following education blogs, joining education chats on social media, attending education conferences, and reading books on education are all tactics that keep you on the cutting edge of the field.

> ➤ **POSITIVE OUTLOOK**

This might sounds simple, however, it can be difficult to have a positive outlook when you are buried under the weight of stress from a hectic school day, week, month… It is important to remember that a positive outlook doesn't mean that everything around you is positive and it won't resolve what is causing you stress. What trying to maintain a positive outlook will do is position you to find solutions, work through issues, and rebound with greater ease. Dealing with stress when all you can see is stressors around you begins a cycle. Negativity breeds negativity, it spirals, and so does positivity. Give yourself permission to be upset when need be, but always try to refocus your perspective toward the positive.

> ➤ **TEACHER MINDSET**

A teacher's mindset is that of a life-long learner. When faced with a challenge, you have a sense that there are more ways than you may know to face it. An educator with a teacher's mindset looks outwardly when dealing with occupational stress. They ask, *Who can I learn from about the obstacles I am facing? Where can I find more information about how to combat this stress?* This mindset is a foundational piece of a resilient approach to a career in education. Understanding that this isn't it, that there is more to be learned, more hope to be found, and more strategies to try is a habit of mind that serves educators well in both dealing with the stresses of their career and approaching challenges in the classroom.

➢ PRIORITIZE

It is almost against the nature of an educator to put themselves first. You need to be a priority. Your health and your life is important and meaningful to those around you. Self-care is not selfish, it is necessary. Placing importance on your own well-being also means making time for those around you. Taking care of yourself means making time to spend with your loved ones, outside of school. So, prioritize and make sure there is some time left each week for those you care about and for yourself.

➢ SCHOOL PROGRAM

Be instrumental in influencing the resilience in your school. Start a committee on teacher well-being/resilience/job satisfaction. Suggest teacher resilience as an in-service topic. Lead a book study (remember for this book there is a *The Definitive Joy in Teaching Workbook*, specifically designed for group work). Become the person that colleagues go to for support. Bring in speakers that encourage and inspire a focus on teacher well-being. Take steps to make your school a place where teachers feel supported and heard.

➢ PROFESSIONAL ASSISTANCE

Sometimes it feels like we have tried everything and the stress is still overwhelming. There are mental-health professionals that can assist. Some school districts have begun to support this step. It doesn't all have to rest on your shoulders.

Moving forward means taking action. Consider the protective practices and resilience strategies and begin to envision them as part of your approach to teaching. Does employing these strategies look different from how you have cared for yourself prior to this book? Remember, your well-being is important, not just to you and your family and friends, but also to your students, their success, and the success of your school as a whole.

Discussion Questions

1. What protective practices stand out to you as necessary in your approach to education?
2. Consider the protective practices you have chosen to implement. How can you transform these practices into habits of your daily life?
3. Are there any protective practices that could become part of a school improvement plan/school-wide initiative? How?

Call to Action

Chapter Overview
- Determine what strategies fit best for you.

- Consider how you know when you are stressed.

- Develop a plan for when you will use your resiliency strategies.

- Remember your purpose.

- Seek the joy in teaching.

The warning signs of stress, which can lead to burnout, only get "louder" the longer you ignore them. It's time to put what we have discussed in this book into practice. If you are following along in *The Definitive Joy in Teaching Workbook,* it is time to fill out your action plan. Those of you who are reading the book, create an action plan on a separate sheet of paper and post it somewhere you will regularly see, perhaps in your classroom or in your planner. This plan is how you will make changes and reclaim the joy in teaching.

YOUR ELEMENTS OF ACTION

As you digest all of the ideas offered in the past two chapters, consider your current position and what tools fit best for you. Which practices do you see as beneficial? Which strategies have you already employed? As we move forward, you will finalize a plan of action that you can rely on to combat the occupational stress associated with a career in education.

Select Your Resiliency Tools

Which resiliency strategies and protective practices will work for you? There's no way to know except by trying. However, some of them stood out to you. Some of them, you knew when you read them, fit. Some maybe you already practice, those too deserve space in your plan of action. Consider all the different tools, strategies, and methods discussed and decide which ones you are going to try.

Develop tiers of resilience strategies, some for when things are going well and others for when stress begins to take hold. Refer back to Chapters Thirteen and Fourteen.

Listen to Yourself

You are the best judge of how things are going. Listen to yourself, to your body and your mind. Often it is as simple as when things are going good, we feel good. But, it is when those early warning signs of stress creep in that we need to be aware so that we can take action.

We can separate recognizing warning signs of stress into two different categories – mental and physical.

➤ You may recognize early warning signs of stress mentally through intuition or instincts - that gut feeling that things aren't right.

154

➤ You may recognize the physical warning signs of stress through the tensing of shoulders, the clenching of teeth, a quickening of breath, or a faster heartbeat.

Stress is normal, it can even be healthy. Stress can alert you to changes and provide a sense of urgency to a task. For some, stress becomes motivation. Living and working with a certain level of stress is okay. It is when you notice the wear of occupation stress, when it feels negative or overwhelming, that it is your signal to make a change. This moment is when new resiliency skills need to be employed. By listening to yourself, you can make the necessary adjustments to your routine quickly and avoid moving down The Teacher Burnout Scale.

Know When to Use Them

Don't wait until you are on the brink of burnout to begin to build your resilience. Certain practices can be a part of your daily routine. Others can be used strategically when you first experience stress before you become overwhelmed.

Develop a plan for when you will use the tools you have chosen. The point here is not to let yourself get to the point that you are not sure what to do. You don't need to feel as if your back is to the wall. Having a plan in place now allows you to move forward knowing that for every scenario, for each step along the Teacher Burnout Scale, you have a counter move. Just as in teaching you want to have a toolbox full of ideas so that you are never unprepared.

Consider what strategies work best when you are feeling slightly stressed, which practices should be part of your routine, what actions you will take when the stress gets louder, and how you will back yourself down the Teacher Burnout Scale when you are feeling depleted or are nearing burnout. How will you take care of yourself when teaching is going great? And, how will you take care of yourself when teaching becomes seemingly too much to handle?

 Ask yourself the tough questions now so that when those hectic school days come, as we know they will, you do not have to think about how you will react.

Remember Why You Started

Write the reason(s) you are an educator down. Put it at the top of your action plan. Make it visible each and every day. This is your guiding force, your true North, the reason you do what you do, and your reason why it is so important to develop a resilient approach to teaching. It has been mentioned before in this book and deserves mentioning again, **you are no good to your students if you let yourself burn out.** It is your responsibility to show up and be the best educator you can for your students and staff. This doesn't happen by itself. You need to be thoughtful in your approach and reflective in your practice. You need to understand what you need and equip yourself with the tools it takes to create change.

Seek Joy

Even on the dimmest day, there is joy in teaching. Some days the joy comes from an engaging class, a successful lesson, administrative recognition, colleague support, the big student "a-ha's", laughter, and love. Those days are great. Other days we have to look for the joy. Some days it is hard to find.

Joy in teaching can be in the little things. A moment to sit down with a quiet student and talk, a quiet lunch, an uplifting conversation with a colleague, or new idea for a lesson.

Taking action against stress and burnout does not mean that you are taking ownership of the origins of the stress. It is essential to keep this in mind as you consider your approach to resilience.

Remember what is not in your control and focus on where you can effect change. Use your action plan. Be a disruptor in the field of education and turn the tables on statistics of teacher burnout and attrition. Understand that you can create a culture of positivity for yourself, even if it doesn't exist around you. Rely on your resilience-building skills and keep your eyes open for the joy, because it is there, every day.

Citations

[1] Ryan, S. V., Pendergast, L. L., Schwing, S., von der Embse, N. P., Saeki, E., & Segool, N. (2017). Leaving the teaching profession: The role of teacher stress and educational accountability policies on turnover intent. *Teaching & Teacher Education,* 661-11.

[2] Goldring, R., Taie, S., & Riddles, M. (2014). Teacher attrition and mobility: Results from the 2012–13 Teacher Follow-up Survey (NCES 2014-077). U.S. Department of Education. Washington, DC: National Center for Education Statistics. http://nces.ed.gov/pubsearch.

[3] Podolsky, A., Kini, T., Bishop, J., & Darling-Hammond, L. (2016). Solving the Teacher Shortage: How to Attract and Retain Excellent Educators. Palo Alto, CA: Learning Policy Institute.

[4] Rumschlag, K. E. (2017). Teacher Burnout: A Quantitative Analysis of Emotional Exhaustion, Personal Accomplishment, and Depersonalization. International Management Review, 13(1), 22.

[5] Carr, T. A. (2017, September 18). What Does It Mean to Live an Examined Life in Education? https://joyinteaching.com/what-does-it-mean-to-live-an-examined-life-in-education/

[6] Sutcher, L., Darling-Hammond, L., & Carver-Thomas, D. (2016). A coming crisis in teaching? Teacher supply, demand, and shortages in the US. *Learning Policy Institute. Retrieved from https://learningpolicyinstitute. org/product/coming-crisis-teaching.*

[7] Carr, T. A. (2017, September 19) The Origin of Joy in Teaching. https://joyinteaching.com/origin-of-joy-in-teaching/

[8] Pedota, P.J. (2015). How can Student Success Support Teacher Self-Efficacy and Retention? *Clearing House, 88*(2), 54-61.

[9] Carr, T. A. (2017, September 21). The Importance and Impact of Teacher Well-Being. https://joyinteaching.com/the-importance-and-impact-of-teacher-well-being/

[10] Oberle, E., & Schonert-Reichl, K.A. (2016). Stress contagion in the classroom? The link between classroom teacher burnout and morning cortisol in elementary school students. *Social Science & Medicine, 159,* 30-37.

[11] Briner, R., & Dewberry, C. (2007). Staff wellbeing is key to school success: A research study into the links between staff well being and school performance. Retrieved from http://www.worklifesupport.com/sites/default/files/uploaded-documents/5902BirkbeckWBPerfSummaryFinal.pdf

[12] Steward, J. (2014). Anxiety is contagious: we must stop the spread. *TES: Times Educational Supplement,* (5116), 38.

[13] Roffey, S. Pupil wellbeing – Teacher wellbeing: Two sides of the same coin? *Educational and Child Psychology, 29*(4), 8-17.

[14] Gray, L., & Taie, S. (2015). Public school teacher attrition and mobility in the first five years: Results from the first through fifth waves of the 2007–08 beginning teacher longitudinal study (NCES 2015–337). U.S. Department of Education. Washington DC: National Center for Educational Statistics.

[15] Bobek, B. (2002). Teacher resiliency: A key to career longevity. ClearingHouse, 75(4), 202 206.

[16] Howard, S., & Johnson, B. (2004). Resilient teachers: Resisting stress and burnout. Social Psychology of Education, 7(3), 399-420.

[17] Greenfield, B.B. (2015). How can teacher resilience be protected and promoted?. Educational & Child Psychology, 32(4), 52-68.

[18] Seidel, A. (2014, July 18). The Teacher Dropout Crisis. Retrieved October 03, 2017, from https://www.npr.org/sections/ed/2014/07/18/332343240/the-teacher-dropout-crisis

[19] Carr, T. A. (2017, October 19). Rise From The Ashes - The Teacher Burnout Scale. Retrieved December 05, 2017, from https://joyinteaching.com/rise-from-the-ashes/

[20] Singer, J. (2012). The teachers ultimate stress mastery guide: 77 proven prescriptions to build your resilience. New York, NY: Skyhorse Pub.

[21] Carr, T. A. (2017, October 05). The Warning Signs and Symptoms of Teacher Burnout. https://joyinteaching.com/warning-signs-and-symptoms-of-teacher-burnout/

[22] Maslach, C., Jackson S.E., Leiter, M.P., Schaufeli, W.B., Schwab, R.L., Maslach Burnout Inventory. Accessed December 05, 2017. http:// www.mindgarden.com/products/mbi.htm.

[23] Carr, T. A. (2017, September 21). Teacher resilience education provides teachers the essential tools to change how they experience occupational stress and reclaim their joy in teaching. https://joyinteaching.com/whats-all-this-about-teacher-resilience/

[24] Carr, T. A. (2017, November 16). The Performance of Teaching And It's Impact On Student Success. https://joyinteaching.com/performance-of-teaching/

[25] Krop, J. (2013). Caring without Tiring. Education Canada, 53(2), 42-47.

[26] Fowler, M. (2015). Dealing with Compassion Fatigue. Education Digest, 81(3), 30-35.

[27] Carr, T. A. (2017, September 18). Go Backward to Move Forward - A Resilience Strategy to Motivate Educators. https://joyinteaching.com/go-backward-to-move-forward/

[28] Scholastic & Bill & Melinda Gates Foundation. (2012). Primary sources 2012: America's teachers on the teaching profession. New York: Scholastic. Retrieved December 7, 2017 from www.scholastic.com/primarysources/pdfs/Gates2012_full.pdf

[29] Carr, T. A. (2017, November 02). It's Time For A Boost - The School Year's Cycle Demands It. https://joyinteaching.com/its-time-for-a-boost/

[30] Carr, T. A. (2017, September 19). How Depressing Statistics on Teaching Deliver Hope. https://joyinteaching.com/howdepressingstatisticsonteachingdeliverhope/

[31] Walker, T. (2015, August 26). NEA Survey: Nearly Half Of Teachers Consider Leaving Profession Due to Standardized Testing. Retrieved March 19, 2017, from http://neatoday.org/2014/11/02/nea-survey-nearly-half-of-teachers-consider-leaving-profession-due-to-standardized-testing-2/

32 Staff, T. (2016, March 27). A Teacher Makes 1500 Educational Decisions A Day. Retrieved March 19, 2017, from http://www.teachthought.com/ pedagogy/teacher-makes-1500-decisions-a-day/

33 Teachers Win Fight For More Planning Time. (2014, November 21). Retrieved March 20, 2017, from http://neatoday.org/2013/10/17/teachers-win-fight-for-more-planning-time-2/

34 Williams, J. (2015, May 15). Survey Reveals That America's Teachers Are Seriously Stressed Out. Retrieved March 20, 2017, from http://www.takepart.com/article/2015/05/15/groundbreaking-survey-reveals-americas-teachers-are-seriously-stressed-out

35 O'Brennan, L. I., Pas, E., & Bradshaw, C. (2017). Multilevel Examination of Burnout Among High School Staff: Importance of Staff and School Factors. *School Psychology Review*, 46(2), 165-176.

36 Holmes, E. (2005). *Teacher well-being*. London: Routledge Falmer.

37 Biro, M. M. (2016, April 18). Happy Employees = Hefty Profits. Retrieved December 12, 2017, from https://www.forbes.com/sites/meghanbiro/2014/01/19/happy-employees-hefty-profits/#629f923e221a

38 Kesler, C. (n.d.). Where Passions Come Alive. Retrieved December 12, 2017, from http://www.geniushour.com/

39 Carr, T. (2017, September 28). What The Business World Figured Out Before Education Did. https://joyinteaching.com/what-the-business-world-figured-out-before-education-did/

40 Doney. P. (2013). Fostering Resilience: A Necessary Skill for Teacher Retention. *Journal of Science Teacher Education*, 24(4), 645-664.

41 Singer, N. R., Catapano, S., & Huisman, S. (2010). The university's role in preparing teachers for urban schools. *Teaching Education,21*(2), 119-130.

42 Shen, Bo; McCaughtry, Nate; Martin, Jeffrey; Garn, Alex; Kulik, Noel; Fahlman, Mariane. *British Journal of Educational Psychology* , Dec2015, Vol. 85 Issue 4, p519-532, 14p, 3 Charts.

43 Hattie, J. (2010). Visible learning: a synthesis of over 800 meta-analyses relating to achievement ;. London: Routledge.

44 Carr, T. A. (2015). Addressing the non-artist's approach to art: A study of pre-service teachers in an art methods course. The University of Iowa.

45 Robinson, K. (2010). Changing education paradigms. RSA Animate, The Royal Society of Arts, London, http://www. youtube. com/watch.

46 Carr, T. A. (2017). The Resilient Teacher's Timesaving Guidebook. https://joyinteaching.com/the-resilient-teachers-timesaving-guidebook/

47 American Psychological Association. (2006, March 20). Multitasking: Switching costs. Retrieved December 15, 2017, from http://www.apa.org/research/action/multitask.aspx

48 Carr, T. A (n.d.). The 10 Types of Resilient Teachers and the Strengths and Struggles of Each. https://joyinteaching.com/the-10-types-of-resilient-teachers-and-the-strengths-and-struggles-of-each

[49] Carr, T.A. (2017, October, 25). What if Teachers Took Their Own Advice? Could It Change How We Teach? https://joyinteaching.com/what-if-teachers-took-their-own-advice/

[50] Vance, A., Pendergast, D., & Garvis, S. (2015). Teaching resilience: a narrative inquiry into the importance of teacher resilience. *Pastoral Care In Education*, *33*(4), 195-204.

[51] Dweck, Carol S. *Mindset: the new psychology of success*. Ballantine Books, 2016.

[52] Carr, T.A. (2017, October, 12). Mindsets, Methods, and Habits: Effect Change Even When You Cant. https://joyinteaching.com/mindsets-methods-and-habits/

[53] Carr, T.A. (2017, September, 22). What's All This About Teacher Resilience Education? And Why It Should Be A Priority in Every Single School. https://joyinteaching.com/whats-all-this-about-teacher-resilience/

[54] Carr, T.A (2017, August, 10). Why Teaching Is The Best (And Worst) Job Ever. https://joyinteaching.com/whyteachingisthebestandworstjobever/

[55] Maslow, A. (1943). A Theory of Human Motivation. *Psychological Review*, 50(4), pp.370-396.

[56] Violence Prevention. (2016, April 01). Retrieved March 08, 2018, from https://www.cdc.gov/violenceprevention/acestudy/index.html

[57] Sutcher, L., Darling-Hammond, L., & Carver-Thomas, D. (2016). A coming crisis in teaching? Teacher supply, demand, and shortages in the US. *Learning Policy Institute*. *Retrieved from https://learningpolicyinstitute. org/product/coming-crisis-teaching*.

[58] Werner, E. E. (1995). Resilience in development. *Current directions in psychological science*, *4*(3), 81-84.

[59] Carr, T.A. (2018, January, 18). 12 Tips to Find the Calm in A Hectic School Day. https://joyinteaching.com/find-the-calm/

[60] Carr, T.A. (2017, August, 10). 8 Tips for Stronger Teacher Resiliency. https://joyinteaching.com/8-tips-for-stronger-teacher-resiliency/

[61] Edwards, C. P., Gandini, L., & Forman, G. E. (2012). The hundred languages of children: The Reggio Emilia experience in transformation. Santa Barbara (California): Praeger.

[62] Carr, T.A. (2018, March, 26). Your Classroom Design Impacts How you Feel About Teaching. https://joyinteaching.com/your-classroom-design-impacts-how-you-feel-about-teaching/

[63] Carr, T.A. (2017, November, 17). Protective Practices and Teacher Well-Being [infographic]. https://joyinteaching.com/protective-practices/

*A*bout *the A*uthor

Dr. Tiffany A. Carr is an experienced leader in education. She has taught in a wide variety of scenarios, led professional development, and spoken at numerous conferences. Her work comes from a place of understanding and support and is fueled by a respect and passion for the education profession. Dr. Carr knows the dynamics of what is happening in our schools and was inspired to write this book as a direct response to the increasing demands and roles of teachers.

For more information about Dr. Tiffany A. Carr,
her professional development offerings, or speaking
presentations visit
www.tiffanycarr.com

If you have enjoyed this book please recommend it to your colleagues and
leave a positive review on www.amazon.com

87964874R00101

Made in the USA
Lexington, KY
04 May 2018